Larkspur

Between the Lines
PUBLISHING

Liminal Books is an imprint of Between the Lines Publishing. The Liminal Books name and logo are trademarks of Between the Lines Publishing.

Between the Lines Publishing
1769 Lexington Ave N., Ste 286
Roseville, MN 55113
btwnthelines.com

Published: April 2023

Original ISBN (Paperback) 978-1-958901-41-0
Original ISBN (eBook) 978-1-958901-42-7

Larkspur

JC Miller

Early praise for *Larkspur*

"*Larkspur* is a heart-aching story of love, friendship, tragedy – life – set in a past that's too easy to forget; fortunately, we have JC Miller to take us back and remind us just how wonderful and hard life can be. Miller puts us in the hearts and minds of three distinct, quirky, delightful characters tied together by love, friendship, and nostalgia. We feel how problems that seem big at the time – a banged up rental car, relationship troubles – disappear in the face of genuine trauma. We feel it, we share it, we're part of it because everyone knows deep inside that tragedy can strike at any moment, and JC Miller puts us right in the center of it." - **Ransom Stephens, bestselling author of *The 99% Solution***

"...you'll laugh, you'll cry, and you'll reluctantly tear yourself away, satisfied... with a heart full of hope." - **Ana Manwaring, author of the award winning JadeAnne Stone Mexico Adventures**

Larkspur is commonly associated with lightheartedness and youth.

—Farmer's Almanac

An old-fashioned annual flower, the larkspur has a variety of symbolic meanings. Most commonly, it is used to symbolize love, affection, and strong attachment.

—Florgeous.com

For Mike

ACT ONE

ACT ONE

Jonathan Wakefield tucked his clean, dry dinner dishes safely into their respective homes, then headed outside for his evening constitutional. He ambled down Parnassus, cut over on Willard, and made his way into Golden Gate Park. On his way home he ducked into a corner market for a pint of milk. Then, to fill the yawning gap before bedtime, and not without a twinge of remorse, he gravitated again to the couch.

With a weary exhale, he clicked the remote and took a spin around the dial. Eventually he landed on *Jeopardy!*, a favorite of Dylan's. As he patted the empty space next to him, he envisioned the little monkey, tangled hair, gangly limbs and all. He smiled faintly, a dry ache in his throat. Then he remembered that today was Wednesday—the most dreaded day of the week since he'd been relegated to "weekend dad" status.

The other weekdays he could abide. On Mondays he taught at the U, and Tuesdays he filled with chores. Thursdays, he set his sights on Fridays, when Kara dropped Dylan off and the world brightened like Oz in technicolor. But Wednesdays were limbo, tinged in gray. Jonathan released an audible sigh, gave the remote a final thumb mash and silenced the TV.

1

Though he'd pretty much sworn off booze, on Wednesdays he made an exception. He poured himself an inch of bourbon, then settled into his study to grapple with the latest draft of his novel. He sipped and pondered, tweaked a sentence here and there. He tasted a cloying sweetness in his mouth, like coming on to LSD—a halo, a tingle foreshadowing inspiration. To coax the muse, he closed his eyes, knowing she was ephemeral and fleeting as a mirage. Words began to take shape in Jonathan's mind as his fingertips flew to the keys. In the same instant, the sound of his doorbell shattered his focus. His jaw tightened.

Damn kids.

The first pimpled male had shown up last week at suppertime. The guy claimed to be earning tuition to Boy's State, and Jonathan, feeling magnanimous, forked over twelve bucks for a year's subscription to *Time*. Less than an hour later, a second chap showed up with his hand out, and like a sucker, Jonathan had again acquiesced. Others followed suit, darkening his door at all hours. Different dudes, same spiel. He'd put his foot down, figured he was rid of them, and for good measure, posted one of those No Solicitation signs.

Jonathan listened intently for the doorbell. He massaged his scalp to quiet his nerves. Hearing only the sounds of his own breath, he returned to his novel to pick up where he'd left off. He commenced the delicate mental untangling, pulling ideas like threads from his memory. Again, the doorbell blared. His blood coursing with rage and adrenaline, he stormed down the hall, yanked the door open and flipped on the porchlight to confront the jerk. As he squinted through the yellowy glare at the man on his stoop, tiny needles of recognition pricked his armpits. Unwanted desire washed over him, rendering him weak-kneed, helpless.

The man spoke. "Hi, Jon."

Jonathan struggled to regain his equilibrium but continued to feel oddly untethered. "Milo?" he managed.

Milo unleashed one of his grins. "Aren't you going to invite me in?"

"Of course, come in," Jonathan said, fumbling with the door.

2

Milo strode in, his vibe nonchalant, like he owned the place. Jonathan pondered the weirdly malleable nature of time and space. How long had it been? Five years at least.

"Nice place," Milo said.

Jonathan studied his former love. The years had clearly been good to him. Milo's thicket of dark curls remained as lush and gorgeous as ever. His body had matured, filled out in all the right places. And those eyes. God help him, he could drown in those brown eyes. Jonathan considered his own graying beard, his paunch—then straightened his posture, sucked in his tum. "How did you find me?" he asked.

Milo swept a curl from his forehead. He grinned. "Long story."

Jonathan had forgotten about the height difference. Feeling diminished, he offered up his reading chair like it was nothing—everything. He took a seat on the couch, opposite Milo. "I've got time."

Milo shrugged. "You're never going to believe it."

Apprehension clung to Jonathan's skin like a damp shirt. "Try me."

"In a word," Milo said, one eyebrow raised, "Kara."

"Kara?"

Milo nodded.

Jonathan couldn't begin to fathom a connection. As far as he was concerned, Milo and Kara did not exist in the same physical sphere. "Kara, as in my ex-wife?"

"The one and only."

Jonathan squinted at him but said nothing.

"She's been letting me use one of her North Beach studios," he explained. "For a few months now."

Over the years, Kara had sponsored a handful of promising artists—not altogether altruistically. If a work sold in one of her galleries, she called it a win-win. "But how?" Jonathan asked, unsure what to say. "How did you happen to meet her?"

Milo exhaled. "Told you, long story."

"As I mentioned, I have time."

"I guess she read some article about me," Milo said, sounding humble. "She liked my work and tracked me down. Called me out of the blue and offered me the studio space, opportunity for exposure."

Jonathan admired Milo's raw talent but thought he lacked drive. With Kara's business acumen, no doubt Milo could go far. "That's fantastic," he said. "But I still don't understand how you made the leap from Kara to me."

"She came by my studio with her son—your son, Dylan. I had a hunch about your connection and Kara confirmed it." He gave Jonathan a pointed look. "Then, I stalked you."

Jonathan's stomach dropped. Throughout his charged, short-lived relationship with Milo, he'd been married to Kara. She'd known about Raj, but he'd never told her about Milo. He'd been a shit husband, and even now, the shame of his betrayal swam in his gut. "Jesus, did you tell her about us?"

"Relax, cowboy. I just told her you were Kit's friend."

Hours later Jonathan reclined on his bed, distracted and wound up. He couldn't quite wrap his mind around Milo's reemergence, seemingly from out of the ether. Yet he had to admit, it was in character. The man always had a penchant for drop-in visits—ambush his forte.

They'd talked well into the night: Milo out of context in Jonathan's wingback reading chair, Johnathan leaning forward on the edge of the couch. They'd spoken of Katherine, or as Milo called her, Kit. The conversation had transported him back to Humboldt State University, a different time and place—a different him. He'd often wondered what had become of Katherine, former student, mentee, and all-around bright spot of his mediocre tenure at HSU. But when he'd pried for updates or knowledge of her whereabouts, Milo had only shrugged, having lost track of her, too.

Neither delved into their own heated past. Sidestepping, he supposed, was part of the dance. It had been late, after two in the morning, when Milo rose to make his departure. There had been a lingering hug at the door, an almost-kiss. The physical longing had caught Jonathan off guard, painfully so. The old emotions, too, had ached in his marrow. He'd been a hair's breadth from surrender, allowing body memory to take over. But in the end, he'd held back, his still-bruised heart unready to open.

New York City
Two Months Later
December 7, 1980

Kit dribbled bubble bath into the stream, emptying the bottle. She removed her laundry day ensemble: baggy sweatshirt and jeans, the ragged cotton underwear with the period stain, and tossed the whole lot to the floor. Finding the water temperature ideal, she gathered her hair into a ponytail and gradually sank into the tub. She leaned back against the shock of cold porcelain and with practiced dexterity grasped the faucet handle between her toes, twisting it to release a trickle of scalding water. She settled back, closed her eyes, and waited for sweet escape.

But *Calgon's* promise to "take her away" failed. She continued ticking checklists, getting her head in the game for Monday morning. To drown out the internal noise, she slipped underwater, releasing her tangle of dark curls to swirl free like mermaid tresses. For a few sweet moments, she let it all go, but when she came up for air, ropes of Sunday night dread knotted up in her guts.

Her job had become intolerable; to feign otherwise, hopeless. In the beginning, she'd convinced herself it would be temporary, a year at most. Powell-Standish, if nothing else, had offered proximity to the literary market— a chance to get her work noticed. Back then, her mind still fizzed with girlish

6

notions. She believed her "real" life would soon begin, like some sleeping princess waiting for a magic frog.

Years piled up. Somewhere along the way, the mind-numbing grind extinguished her spark, as she relegated her own writing to the eternal back burner. Her East Village apartment had lost its charm. Plodding up four flights of stairs with groceries had lost its novelty. Kit felt trapped in a life she'd outgrown.

She'd tried leaving PS, following the want ads, plotting her exit nearly every day. The fucking hell of it was: jobs in her field had dried up. She couldn't just quit—she had rent to pay. And after working all day, her energy drained, she felt paralyzed, defeated before she'd even started. Kit surrendered to her fate, attempting to make the best of it. She'd tried socializing with colleagues, even dated a few.

When loneliness crept in and left her hollowed out, she'd trolled the bars in search of . . . what? Comfort? The latest in a string of inappropriate men, the thick-headed Kevin had finally quit calling. She admitted she'd driven him away. Still, she kind of missed him, his absence spotlighting her isolation. Since her breakup with Joe, Kit still hadn't found anyone who compared. With each unsuitable guy, each failed relationship, a little part of her died. What if she never bounced back?

The phone had been silent all weekend. Now the sound jarred her. *Who in the hell would call after eleven—on a Sunday?* No doubt a nutcase, pervert, or wrong number. She would ignore it.

But then again, it could be Joe. He'd called her that one time, out of the blue. Though he'd claimed he needed a mutual friend's address, she wondered if it had been a pretense.

Kit extracted herself from the tub, hit the light switch, snatched a towel, and stumbled into the bedroom. "Hello?" she breathed, her heart a snare drum.

"Hi sweetie."

No. Not Joe. A tiny flicker of hope fizzled, then died.

"Sorry to call so late."

"Cindy?"

"Yes, I'm sorry. Did I wake you?"

Cindy, her dad's wife, *never* called. Why did her tone sound so strained and weirdly evasive? Glancing at the alarm clock on her nightstand, she confirmed the late hour, after eleven here in New York, about 8:10 in California. Dripping and shivering in her towel, the bottom fell out of Kit's stomach. "No, I'm up," she said. "What's going on?"

"I have news."

"News?"

"It's your dad. He's in the hospital."

Kit sank onto her bed. She wrapped her down comforter around her shoulders, but the chill seeped through her skin all the way to her bones. "What happened?"

"He had a minor heart incident yesterday."

Heart incident? "My God, what do you mean?"

"A very mild heart attack."

Kit's anger flared. "Why didn't you call me?"

Cindy let out a weary breath. "I'm sorry. I wanted to, but you know how he is. Even in the throes of it, he made me promise. He didn't want to upset you."

Kit's vision tunneled. "Upset me? He's my father, for Christ's sake."

"I know."

"Jesus, is he going to be okay?" *He had to be okay because Kit could not lose him. Without him, she would not exist.*

"He's okay, honey. The doctor said he came through the surgery like a champ. He's out of the woods now, so nothing to worry about."

Her stepmom's saccharine tone hit a nerve. She wasn't a child, after all.

Cindy pressed on. "Kathy? Are you still there? Honey?"

Kit struggled to find words. She'd missed Christmas—again. A last-minute ski trip with a man she'd known for precisely three days had waylaid long-held holiday plans with her father. Her father, her rock. The man who loved her unconditionally, the man who would gladly take a bullet for her, lay in some hospital bed.

And where was she?

8

Kit rose to her feet, gripped the receiver like a life preserver and found her voice. "I'm coming home."

San Francisco

The Following Day

Jonathan crammed coins into the parking meter, then sprinted up Lexington. He stopped to catch his breath in front of the nondescript brick school. A small group of parents milled about the entrance. He zeroed in on Kara and Kent chatting with a petite frizzy-haired woman. Kara wore a loose-fitting calico midi dress, her dark hair woven into a braid. His ex-wife had always been a looker, but in the pale afternoon light, she absolutely glowed.

As Jonathan cut across the lawn, a distinctive sound floated on the breeze. A joyful cacophony of children's shouts, footfalls, and bouncing balls washed over him in waves, transporting him to grade school. A remembrance of crisp fall Minnesota mornings, free from self-consciousness. Golden years, before adolescence nailed a target to his back.

Kent stood at the top of the stairs, which further accentuated his height. Jonathan joined Kara on a lower step, taking a glance at his wristwatch. "Phew. I thought I was going to be late."

Kara gave his shoulder a squeeze. "You're right on time." She turned to address the frizzy woman on her left. "Willow, do you know Jon, Dylan's dad?"

Willow's face lit up. "No, I haven't had the pleasure."

Jonathan bristled inwardly at the name *Willow*. He knew the type: typical quasi hippy, clueless California granola-head. Mandatory Birkenstocks, dyed muslin peasant garb, the absence of makeup. A disquieting number of his MFA grad students had also succumbed to this particular version of lockstep conformity. He extended his hand. "Nice to meet you," he said.

She took his hand in both of hers, holding it a bit longer than socially conventional. "It's so nice to meet you, Jon."

Was she flirting? "It's Jonathan," he said.

"Well, Jonathan, I must tell you, your son is extraordinary. Dylan's bright and inquisitive," Willow said, then paused to take a breath. "He's kind, so patient with the little ones."

Kent chimed in. "Willow teaches kindergarten. Dylan's fourth-grade class reads with their kinder buddies on Fridays."

Willow smiled at Kent. "Yes, Kent's one of our Friday parent helpers."

Why Kent's volunteerism rankled him, Jonathan could not be certain. He nodded. "Ah."

Willow gushed on. "I believe Dylan is an old soul, mature and thoughtful beyond his years."

Had Jonathan been too hasty in his judgment of Willow? Perhaps her expertise in child development compensated for her effusive manner and lack of fashion sense. "I can't disagree," he said. "He's a great kid."

Kent draped a lazy territorial arm around Kara's shoulder. Conventionally handsome for a man in his fifties—granite chin, lavish salt-and-pepper hair, ramrod straight spine—he and Kara made an attractive pair. Glancing at him, Jonathan experienced a reflexive twinge of jealousy. Aware of his knee-jerk irrationality, he shook it off. He didn't particularly like Kent, but he'd grown to respect the guy.

A shrill bell cut through Jonathan's thoughts. He looked on as the little kids dashed from the playground, the bigger kids coolly sauntered.

"Enjoy your tour," Willow said before her hasty departure.

Kent held the door open. "Shall we?"

Jonathan hung back, allowing Kara and a few other parents to pass. He'd known what to expect at Dylan's traditional public school, for better or worse.

But here, in Waldorf land, where novelty reigned, he felt a bit lost. For Dylan's sake he'd keep an open mind.

He entered and surveyed the classroom from the bank of tall windows to the children's art projects on display. His gaze fell to the buzzing clump of youngsters sitting cross-legged on the rug, a hive of potential energy, giggles barely contained. He spotted Dylan immediately, the blue jacket and untamed cowlick a giveaway. Jonathan also recognized Zeke, Dylan's new sidekick.

Mr. Patrick raised a hand, summoning silence. He welcomed the families, uttered a few generalities, then set the classmates free.

Dylan scrambled from the rug to his people. Enduring a public hug from Kara, his cheeks reddened. "Ready for the tour?" he asked.

Jonathan smiled but refrained from hugging him. "You bet."

The tour began with Dylan methodically removing objects from his desk. From his favorite hot dog pencil eraser to his original pen-and-ink rendering of Tolkien's fictional universe, he explained each item's significance. Dylan showed them his California history project, his library books and graded papers. Jonathan had been especially impressed with the boy's study of binary mathematics.

Next, they toured the music room. Dylan showed them the instrument cupboard where he stored his violin. He enthused about his solo in the upcoming concert. They toured the art room, the playground, the lunch tables before circling back to the classroom. No stone unturned.

Mr. Patrick thanked them all for coming. With school over for the day, they made their way outside to the lawn.

"Fantastic tour," Kent offered.

Dylan's expression revealed both humility and pride. "Thanks," he said. Then he tugged Jonathan's shirt. "Did you like it, Dad?"

For unknown reasons, Jonathan's eyes misted. "I loved it." He scooped the boy into his arms. "We're so proud of you," he said into Dylan's ear.

Dylan threw his small arms around Jonathan's neck, held on tight. "See you Friday, Poppy."

Jonathan kissed his cheek. "See you Friday, monkey."

12

Dylan loosened his grip, and after an ungainly slide down Jonathan's limbs, landed on his feet.

Kara tousled his hair. "Ready to get going?"

Dylan shrugged. "Can we get ice cream?"

Kara chuckled. "Sure thing, kiddo."

They set out in the opposite direction of Jonathan's parked car, toward their home. With a painful swallow, he watched the three of them ambling down the sidewalk like a picture.

Jonathan wouldn't have missed it for the world, but today's visit to Dylan's school had taken a toll. His shoulders felt tight, his body heavy with fatigue. To recalibrate and work out the kinks, he ripped open a five-pound sack of flour. He dipped a hand into the sack, running his fingers through the polished grain, cool and silky to the touch. With a careful eye, he measured cups of flour into the bubbly sourdough starter, working it in with his hands. Dumping the mixture onto the butcher's block, he realized he needed to sprinkle in more flour. As he stretched and folded the dough into shape, he thought about life's twists and turns, destiny, kismet.

Somehow the universe sent Milo back at precisely the right moment, his dogged presence a balm for Dylan's absence. Since Milo's surprise appearance two months ago, they'd been nearly inseparable. The second time around, as it turned out, was even sweeter. Milo's persistence, like raindrops on limestone, gradually eroded Jonathan's resistance. Milo had blown all his covers, and for the first time in his wretched life, Jonathan felt seen.

He let out a lengthy exhale. Despite his lifelong habit of self-sabotage, when it came to romance, it seemed his time had finally come. Once again, oddly, he owed his good fortune to Kara. He shuddered to think where he'd be without her. Kara more than anyone had influenced his life in multiple ways and for the better. At a primal level, without Kara there would be no Dylan. And it had been Kara who'd discovered Milo's so-called "outsider" art. Unwittingly, she'd paved his way to San Francisco and to Jonathan.

The irony of Kara's blessing was not lost on him. He knew he'd failed her as a husband; he'd been a chronic liar and a drunk. Yet she'd kept their marriage intact, patching walls, shoring up the foundation. He'd left so many clues, no doubt hoping to be caught. But the woman never quit until it crumbled all around her. Even Kara couldn't ignore the obvious. Her husband had a male lover: her husband was gay. Kara had been furious at first. Then, to his surprise, her fury turned to relief. She'd sprung to life like a kid on the first day of summer vacation.

In stark contrast to his ex-wife's reaction, after the breakup Jonathan had felt ashamed and exposed. He'd spent several subsequent weeks moping, drinking, and wallowing in self-pity. It had been Kara who'd prodded him to get over it, to get off his sorry ass and rebuild his relationship with Dylan.

Kara, too, had nudged him to move closer to his son, and it turned out to be the best decision of his life. In San Francisco he'd found sanctuary. His first wobbly steps as an openly gay man into the notorious Castro District had been enlivening, faltering, and even terrifying at times. In the end, he'd shied away from the uninhibited throng. Jonathan's midwestern values ran deep. *You could take the boy out of Minnesota, but you couldn't take Minnesota out of the boy,* or something akin. The West Coast's radical gay ethos, though intriguing, didn't fit. He lacked the desire to frequent gay haunts, dance bare-chested, party all night, or fuck indiscriminately.

His move to the city had been about giving up the disguise, not replacing it. Yes, he identified as gay, and happily so, but to disregard his nature would have been a regression. Jonathan accepted, even *liked* the person he'd become: a reserved, somewhat square dad. He desired the conventional, boring stuff, like monogamy and family. A romantic at heart but a pragmatist in practice, he'd figured the odds were against him.

Giving up on love, he'd simply focused on the business of living. He'd concentrated on making a home, being a good dad, finishing his next novel. Eventually he took a part-time faculty job at the University of San Francisco leading graduate seminars. In time, he'd collected a small circle of friends. Sure, it would have been nice to find Mr. Right, but he wasn't holding his breath. So, when Milo blew back into his life, he hadn't been expecting love.

He shook his head, remembering. As he placed the dough ball into a big ceramic bowl, he covered it with a clean cotton towel, tucked it in as he would

14

a baby. He pictured Milo bumping through the kitchen door, the heady scent of fresh-baked bread a seduction. Soon they would dine on rare steak, spinach salad, warm, crusty bread with butter—and each other.

New York City
December 8, 1980
That Same Day

"Why the hell did I come to work?" Kit muttered under her breath. She'd meant to tie up a few loose ends before her flight, but thus far had accomplished zero, unless she counted monitoring the sluggish second hand of the wall clock. She reread a paragraph for the zillionth time, then her vision glazed. Her gaze fell to her desktop, where she tracked the movement of an ant no more than a speck with legs. The speck moved purposefully as if it knew the terrain well, rounding her Powell-Standish logo mug and pen jars. It dodged the Fresca can, no doubt too savvy for artificial sugar. Next it scaled the ancient photo of her with Joe, a dusty desktop fixture that had become all but invisible to her.

Kit monitored the ant as it wielded an Oreo crumb twice its size down the desk leg and onto the carpet. Onward it staggered before vanishing into a wall crack, presumably returning to its ant overlord. If memory served, an adult ant possessed the ability to carry five times its own weight. Ah, the trivial little facts she still remembered from biology class. Senior year—the year she met Joe. Kit bit her lip hard, holding back the memories.

Turning back to her work, her mind drifted again to the previous night's ordeal. For hours she'd tried to reach Pan Am reservations, only to get a busy

16

signal. Overwhelmed with worry and restless as a caged beast, she'd indiscriminately shoved clothing into her suitcase, stared at the TV, and finished off a carton of mint-chip ice cream, a hunk of jack cheese, and a box of stale saltines. She'd slept briefly, waking with a start at six o'clock. Finally getting through to the airline, she booked a seat on tonight's redeye. Her brain felt cottony, her head so heavy she could barely hold it up.

Stealing a glance at her officemate, Bradley, Kit felt the old resentment balling up like a wad of gum in her gut. Compared to her gritty little ant buddy, Bradley's work ethic paled. She groaned, perhaps a bit too loudly, recalling the good old days when her office had been private, her desk tidy. At Greene, the most satisfying aspect of her job had been working directly with authors. At Powell-Standish, she'd been reduced to a go-between. Stuck in a windowless office, screening backlogged submissions, she imagined her brain cells shrinking. The recent hire of Bradley added insult to injury.

Her glower fixed on the slush pile, a logic-defying heap that never shrank. She imagined the muffled wail of forsaken bottom dwellers, the stories buried alive. With a pang of guilt, she admitted she'd shuffled a few to the bottom of the pile, a few straight into the bin.

Kit confronted the six-hundred-page manuscript, the embodiment of her woe and sole reason she'd bothered to come to the office today. Having meant to take it home over the weekend, in her usual Friday rush she'd left it behind. On Friday, it had impressed her for some reason, but flipping through the pages now, she questioned her judgment.

Why hadn't she called in sick? Why hadn't she simply lied, like everyone else? But no. Good old Kit, follower of rules—good old Kit, conscientious to a fault. Slacking was not in her DNA. Bradley, however, was hardwired for slack.

She watched as he clacked away on his typewriter, oblivious to her glare, hammering out another canned rejection with mechanical glee. He signed the letter, sealed it in a company-issued white envelope, and affixed the proper postage. Satisfied with a job well done, he propped his feet up on his desk and reached for his rumpled pack of Merits.

He turned to Kit. "Where does your dad live?"

"Pacifica."

He gave her a blank look.

"Near San Francisco," she clarified.

"Did Donna give you sick days?" he asked.

Despite Kit's heroic attendance record, in response to her legit request for time off, Donna, the troll in personnel, had given her a skeptical head tilt. Kit had been required to submit a pound of flesh, fill out a load of paperwork, and sign in blood. After much hand wringing, Donna granted her measly leave. "A week," Kit said.

"When's your flight?" Bradley asked, his tone revealing fading interest.

"Tonight." She checked her watch. "In six hours, seventeen minutes."

Bradley nodded. He loosened his tie, leaned back in his chair, and lit a cig. "Shit. I guess you'd better get cracking." He smiled at her, amused with his own wit.

Bradley's camera-ready, choreographed cool guy image irked her—the narrow tie, the sandy Beach Boys' haircut coifed perfectly messy, black-framed glasses smartening him up. The stench of his smoke drifted into Kit's breathing space. "You do know those things will kill you, right?"

Bradley tapped his ash into a used Coke can, grinning smugly. "No, not these—they're low tar."

Idiot.

A gnarly fist of rancor jabbed at her insides. Kit had trained Bradley. However, via Liz in accounting—the most reliable source of office gossip— she'd learned his entry-level salary outmatched her current pay. Kit suspected they were grooming him for a promotion. With her luck, he'd probably end up being her boss.

She worked her finger into the ragged cuff of her angora sweater. What an unjust morning it had been. Squeezing into the dank, standing-room-only subway car a split second before it rumbled away, Kit had planted her feet firmly, only to be jostled and shoved at every stop. She'd trudged up the stairs, emerging from the city's underbelly exhausted, and rather than lugging her suitcase six blocks to the office, decided to treat herself to a cab. Big mistake. Like a metal claw at the penny arcade, the door handle had bitten into her sleeve, unraveling fistfuls of blue angora. Unraveling Kit.

18

Her workday finally over, Kit braved the train to JFK and holed up in the dim airport lounge. Staring blankly at the latest copy of *Ms.*, she nibbled onion rings, avoiding eye contact with the foxy bartender on duty. When he approached her, she blurted the first cocktail that sprang to mind. "I'll have a tequila sunrise," she said, surprising herself.

It arrived in a tall icy glass, a pretty lava lamp of a drink with striations of red and orange, a fluorescent maraschino cherry floating on top. She took a first tentative sip and found it sickly sweet. But the more she drank, the more it grew on her. She dunked an onion ring into the ketchup pooling on her plate. It tasted of salt and grease, delicious. Washing it down with a gulp of sunrise, she considered her glass, nearly empty now. Kit weighed the benefits and pitfalls of ordering a second.

The bartender, who may have been a mind reader, returned. "Can I get you another?" he asked, his vibe flirtatious.

With his shaggy black hair, rumpled white shirt, and necktie askew, he was one of those disheveled guys who managed to look hot. Emboldened by tequila, she looked him in the eye, toying with the naughty notion of accepting another drink. "No thanks," she said.

He grinned. "What's a nice girl like you doing in a dump like this?"

She flirted a little, giggled at his quip. But after he was gone, his question lingered. What *was* she doing in this dump? Grief lumped in her throat. She blotted her eyes with the bar napkin, remembering her dad.

Now her plate resembled the aftermath of a grisly accident, pale-red ketchup juices mingling with the greasy debris from her onion rings. She pushed it away. Kit glanced at her watch and gathered her belongings, pausing to leave a few dollars on the table. As a veteran of Waffle Hamlet, tipping wait staff was never optional.

Exiting the darkened bar, she squinted into the pulsating fluorescent terminal. Her own pulse kept pace with the frenetic atmosphere as she glided past the bookshop, the I ♥ NY store, the shoeshine kiosk. But she hit a bottleneck outside a sports bar. Bodies spilled out onto the concourse, no doubt straining to glimpse some idiotic football homerun. She nudged and pushed her way through the throng, like a true New Yorker, when a chilling realization hit. This was not a crowd of rabid sports fans, but a grave, sober assembly. She turned to the woman next to her. "What's going on?"

The woman's expression clouded with anguish and disbelief. "John Lennon is dead."

Kit hustled down the seemingly endless corridor, arriving moments before takeoff. A harried-looking stewardess bustled her aboard, telling her to sit anywhere. She spotted her opening at the rear of the aircraft in the last vacant row. The engine rumbled and vibrated as the plane roared down the runway. Kit collapsed into her seat with a groan of relief. She glanced out her window and observed the city lights below until they gradually disappeared into the void. Kit experienced a sudden longing for earthly clay, to plant her feet on solid ground. In her solitary seat, she felt uneasy and apart, frightened.

Had she heard correctly? John Lennon, dead?

No. Not possible. John Lennon *could not* be dead. John Lennon was a Beatle. He lived in New York at the Dakota, not far from Powell-Standish. In fact, Bradley claimed he'd spotted him in Central Park—recently, perhaps a week ago, at lunchtime. Just a normal dad, with his little boy riding on his shoulders. Her gut told her the woman in the airport had been right.

People died. Her dad could have died. Fuck. Was she too late? Was her dad going to live? She closed her eyes, but could not shut out her fears, the questions swimming in her head.

A flight attendant with a high ponytail and a tight smile interrupted Kit's contemplation. She gratefully accepted a foil bag of salted peanuts, a tiny vodka bottle, a miniature can of tonic water, and a plastic cup filled with ice. As she twisted the top from her tiny vodka, Kit smiled at the absurdity of life, this never-ending hard day's night.

The plane landed in San Francisco around five in the morning. On zero sleep and groggy from her flight, Kit made her way to the shuttered Hertz counter. By six fifteen, she found herself behind the wheel of a boxy Toyota Corolla, rolling out of the airport parking garage into the bright California morning. Kit glued her eyes to the road. She knew how to get from the airport to her dad's "beach shack" in Pacifica (a far cry from dusty Trona, as he liked to say), but today the route was unfamiliar, San Francisco a maze. Cindy's directions to the cardiac trauma center were sketchy at best.

Despite her best efforts to concentrate on her driving, Kit managed to make a series of wrong turns, landing on Van Ness in a chaotic thicket of full-blown San Francisco madness. Between the blare of honking horns and her heartbeat thrumming in her ears, Kit couldn't hear herself think. Sensibly, she pulled over at the corner Shell station.

She dug through the rental's glove compartment, finding an owner's manual, a pack of cherry Life Savers, a Hertz brochure, and no map. As she muttered expletives, her eyes filled with idiotic tears. Now she'd have to buy a damn map, and gas stations always jacked up the price. Travel weary and sick of her shitty-shitty life, exhaustion pressed down on her shoulders.

Kit raised her sorry head, turning her gaze to a bus stop shelter across the street. There, she spotted a woman, head bowed as if in prayer. With apparent reverence, the woman placed a handful of daisies at an altar overflowing with flowers of every hue. Kit realized she'd stumbled upon an impromptu memorial. At the heart of the shrine, a framed poster of John Lennon. She rolled down her window to get a better look. Lennon's familiar lyrics poured through the tinny speakers and drifted through her window, directly into her very core.

The song carried her back to her college days at Humboldt. After closing Waffle Hamlet for the night, she and her goofy best friend, Milo, a huge Lennon fan, had often blasted his records. To let off steam while cleaning up, they'd dance around the restaurant, singing at the top of their lungs like a pair of lunatics. Milo always could make her cut loose, make her crack up. She wondered about him now. The memory made her smile, but there was tightness in her chest, a pain like homesickness for a place that no longer existed, one to which she could never return. Why had they drifted apart? There'd been a hasty postcard from Amsterdam—two years ago—and that was the last she'd heard from him. She missed the organic friendship they'd shared, those innocent days before the "real world" hit. The real world, as it turned out, sucked.

Ronald Reagan had won the election—the first blow. Now John Lennon had been shot dead. She could not deny a very real seismic shift in the universe, perhaps the very last drop of idealism draining from her body. But there was no time to grieve, no time to mourn its passing. Her father needed her. And here she sat in some gas station, utterly lost. Kit hung her head in defeat, tears filling her eyes and spilling over.

Kit headed past the bank of gas pumps into the station's service center. The garage reeked of black rubber tires, tobacco, and sweat, manly scents that made her slightly woozy. She spotted the attendant, a hippy type with a rangy straw-colored ponytail, tinkering with a car up on hydraulic jacks. "Excuse me," she said in a loud voice. "I'd like to buy a map."

He tossed his wrench to the workbench and wiped his hands on a dirty rag. "You lost?"

Kit exhaled audibly. "Sort of."

Taking a closer look, she noticed he wore coveralls with the name *Ben* embroidered on his breast pocket. She judged him minimally harmless, probably not a rapist, but dug her hands into her pockets and grasped her car keys in her fist, just in case.

Ben grabbed a map from the rack and spread it out on the countertop. "Where you headed?"

"Saint Francis Hospital. Cardiac center."

He nodded.

Kit detected a knowing look on Ben's face. She wondered about his connection to the hospital. A sick friend, perhaps? Then again, she might have imagined it.

Running a grease-stained finger along the map, he pointed out their location. "Just make a hard right at the signal. Then it's three blocks to the parking garage on your left."

Tension drained from her body. Three or four blocks, doable. She thanked Ben for his trouble and bought a pack of Dentyne to even things out.

An invisible thread must have guided her from the airport through the baffling labyrinth of San Francisco. She'd landed at the Shell station—not the bull's eye, but damn close to the target. Kit had always questioned God's existence, but in this case had to give him (or her) credit.

As she made her way into the belly of the hospital parking structure, she felt a second wind coming on. The elevator door pinged open, bringing a filmy memory to the surface: the last time she'd set foot in a hospital, nearly twenty years ago, when she'd had a tonsillectomy. The operation had come on the heels of her parents' marriage dissolving, her mother's leaving. She recalled a moment of terror and the sound of her own silent scream before the cloying perfumed ether drowned her in a vaguely purple ocean of sleep. She'd woken up disoriented, longing for a mother's comfort, her throat raw and aching.

With a painful swallow, Kit followed the signs up to ICU. She located her dad's corner room and tentatively poked her head in the door. The room held a complicated landscape of gleaming medical devices, but inconceivably, the bed lay empty. Her mind hurtled to the most dreaded conclusion.

"Can I help you, hon?"

Kit pivoted on her heels, coming face to face with a woman in olive scrubs. She looked straight into her weary eyes. "Where's my dad?"

The woman squinted at her. "Do you mean Mr. Hilliard?"

"Yes!"

"Transferred him this morning, just a few hours ago. Fifth floor."

Released from ICU—this was good news, right? Kit frowned. "What room?"

A dizzying cocktail of relief and dread churned in her bowels, or maybe it was the airline vodka. With a trembling finger, she called the elevator, changed her mind, and bolted up multiple flights of stairs. She made her way to the end of a long corridor, where she found her dad's room, the door ajar. She peeked in and caught him unawares, reading the newspaper. Scrutinizing her father's appearance, she decided that other than a slight pallor, he looked normal—entirely like himself. "Hey, Daddy," she called.

He glanced up, a smile lighting his face. "Kathy."

Kit glided to his bedside and gave him a careful, not-too-tight hug. "How are you feeling?"

He smiled, the crinkles around his eyes deepening. "I'm fine—just fine."

The pale green gown he wore exposed his farmer's tan. Kit smiled at this. She studied him in search of abnormality or cause for alarm. "You look good," she concluded.

"You, too, sweetie. You sure are a sight for these old eyes. But as you can see, you really didn't need to come."

Kit glanced down at her father's big hands, work-worn and dry. She loved those hands. "Dad, of course I came."

"Well, I wish you hadn't gone to all that trouble. I know how busy you are with work and all."

Her face scrunched. "You know, you just had a heart attack."

"A mild one, practically nothing," he said. "They're sending me home today."

Taking in her father's washed-out complexion, she doubted the decision to release him today. "Really? So soon?"

"Yep. I'm doing fine. The doctor ordered moderate exercise and a low-cholesterol diet, which I'm sure Cindy will enforce like a drill sergeant."

On cue, Cindy showed up, paper cup in hand. "I heard that, Don." She gave Kit a wry smile, set her cup down on the bedside tray, and wrapped her in a mama bear hug.

Kit had almost forgotten about her stepmom's crushing hugs, her grounding presence. "It's good to see you," she murmured, hugging her back.

Cindy fluffed her husband's pillow, then smiled at Kit. "Thank you so much for coming, honey. I'm so glad you're here."

Kit looked pointedly at her father. "Well, you're in the minority."

Cindy gave her a knowing eye roll. "Don't listen to him," she said. "He was thrilled when I told him you were coming. Now that you're here, I think I'll run home for a bit and do a few chores, take a shower. And I'll pick up some fresh clothes for you, Don."

Kit noted the weariness in Cindy's eyes. "Take your time," she said.

Cindy kissed her husband's cheek. "See you in a bit."

"Maybe try to get some rest," Kit said. "I'll be here with Dad." But even as she said it, Kit knew Cindy's devotion would not allow her to rest. It had taken Kit a while to warm to her dad's wife. As a lifelong daddy's girl, she admitted, she'd been a little jealous at first. Her opinion changed as she witnessed her dad's transformation from melancholic bachelor to contented married man.

Kit's so-called real mom split when she was a little kid. Her father stepped up, his steadfast presence her anchor. Kit had never felt lacking. Still, sometimes she wondered how her life might have turned out if she'd had a solid mom like Cindy.

With Cindy's departure, Kit moved closer to her father. "Can I get you anything? A drink or maybe a snack?"

"I'm a little tired, honey," he said. "Mind if we just watch TV for a little while?"

"Of course," Kit said. She flipped on the TV and tuned into a hockey game. "Is this okay?"

Her dad smiled. "That's good."

Kit shoved her chair a bit closer, one eye on the game, when she noticed activity out in the hallway. A woman in business attire walked by, followed by a man in scrubs, their pace brisk and intentional. Her stomach fluttered with recognition. She'd seen that man before, but where? The face of the mechanic from the Shell station, Ben, sprang to her mind unbidden. Kit chalked it up to exhaustion, her weary mind playing tricks.

San Francisco
A Few Days Later

Jonathan relaxed into his favorite armchair by the window, anticipating two of life's greatest pleasures: a cup of black java and the *Chronicle*. He glanced outside at the rain-drenched sidewalk, took a sip of restorative brew and set his cup down on the windowsill. Opening the "Nation" section with a snap, he began scanning the headlines. Mark David Chapman, John Lennon's assassin, had made the front page—again. Evidence revealed the murder had been premeditated; indeed, Chapman may have been planning it for months. Beyond all reason, this delusional young man altered the course of human history. Jonathan's expression darkened. How the media loved an antihero.

He and Milo had joined the candlelight vigil on the polo field in Golden Gate Park. Glancing at fellow mourners, he'd added yet another reason to count himself lucky for living in such a fine city. San Francisco, unlike anywhere else, was an enclave of tolerance. Jonathan had glanced at Milo, heartbroken and in shock, weeping openly. He'd wrapped his arms around him, holding him, kissing him in front of God and everyone as fear drained from his body like water. In that moment he fell more deeply in love. He knew Milo was the one.

Unlike Milo, Jonathan hadn't been able to shed a tear. His emotions, delayed as usual, came later when he'd spoken to Dylan on the phone. He'd envisioned John's young son waking up fatherless, and his heart shattered. His little boy's voice cut through him, making him shudder. There but for the grace of God, he'd thought, considering his own fragile, tenuous life.

Jonathan folded the paper and set it aside. Lennon's death struck him as a turning point, like the Kennedy assassination, forever etched in the collective memory. Here in San Francisco's microculture, among the progressive and likeminded, he imagined life would continue to make sense. But with Reagan's recent election, he feared the rest of the country was reeling, swerving down a precarious path. He no longer recognized the United States he thought he'd understood. He'd wept for John's son, for all of humanity, all the senseless bullshit. But there had been no catharsis, no relief. Only questions.

registered in a serious tone. It's up to us now, Kit had heart shattered. The little boy's voice had broken himself through the firestopped. There but for the grace of God he is limited, considering his own tragic fashion, but...

Sunday, December 13, 1980
Two Days Later
Pacifica, California

Kit glanced out the window as the morning mist turned to drizzle. She spooned the last bite of oatmeal into her mouth, making an effort. She'd never been much of a breakfast person and after a solid week of oats found herself craving a big plate of bacon and scrambled eggs.

Cindy took a sip of juice and cleared her throat to break the silence. "You're all packed?"

Kit nodded. "Yep."

Her dad glanced at her over his glasses. "When's your flight, honey?"

"9:10."

"I guess you'd better get going." He met her eyes. "Seems like you just got here."

He was right. The week had evaporated. She observed him pretending to scan the morning headlines as if it were any ordinary day, as if their parting didn't hurt. But Kit saw through the ruse and put on her game face, too—because that's what grownups did.

The page had turned, and there would be no turning back. She had officially entered the adult world. Her father was no longer her personal Helios, guardian of her well-being, but a mortal man, after all. And their roles were changing, whether she liked it or not. Kit vowed to set childhood illusions aside, to be a better daughter, come what may. If this week had been a test, she figured she'd passed.

After springing him from the hospital and getting him settled in at home, Kit and Cindy joined forces. Their mission: to rid the house of potential hazards. Chocolate ripple ice cream, potato chips, butter, bacon—in short, anything with flavor. If her father mourned the loss of his favorite foods, he didn't mention it. He never once complained but embraced the new regimen as if it were sport, downing daily medications, eating oatmeal and veggies, cutting out salt.

Kit had accompanied her dad on his daily walks around the neighborhood. Each day they ventured a little farther, often winding up at the shore. The salt air rejuvenated him, reviving the color in his cheeks. Taking in the rugged beauty of the California coastline, she, too, sensed her own healing.

Kit stole a glance at her dad and confirmed he looked well, perhaps better than he had in years. She attributed his recovery to his solid character, his salient will to live. This had deepened her respect for him. It had also reassured her; her dad had no intention of checking out any time soon. Still, it would not be easy to say goodbye this time. She considered returning to New York while her dad remained in California—so far away it might as well be the moon.

Her head buzzing with nervous energy, she checked her watch for the third time in the last five minutes. Her midafternoon arrival at JFK left little wiggle room before work on Monday morning. To stir her anxiety pot, she ran down her pre-work checklist. She'd need to catch the train from JFK, catch a cab to her dry cleaners and neighborhood market. Then it dawned on her— today was Sunday and everything would be closed by five. Shit.

Her dad folded his paper and set it on the table. "Ready?"

Kit snapped out of it. "Ready as I'll ever be."

He smiled, reached over, and patted her hand. "We'll walk you out."

Never a fan of prolonged goodbyes, Kit pushed through her emotions. There were the usual bear hugs, the promises to return soon. As she pulled out of the driveway and turned down the street, she glanced back at her father, still waving goodbye. Her strong dad looked smaller, frailer in his flannel bathrobe. Kit swallowed her sorrow and focused on the road.

After a week with her sedate parents, the wider world struck her as clamorous and oddly foreign. But as she merged into the heavy airport traffic, it all came crashing back. The sudden memory of John Lennon's death hit. An event, she realized, that would forever remain seared into her consciousness. She envisioned the makeshift memorial, the outpouring of grief, music drifting on the fog, haunting and exquisite. An ordinary bus stop, an altar.

As Kit drew closer to the airport rental car return garage, her brain commanded her to enter. But her heart had other ideas. For reasons she didn't understand, she veered into the steady stream of SFO departures traffic. No problem. She'd simply circle back, drop the car and board her flight on time.

Thoughts streaked across her mental canvas, blurred and muddied like watercolors. What did she have to come home to? No boyfriend, no prospects, not even a cat. She pictured the dormant apartment awaiting her, milk curdling in her fridge, the unmade bed. Come Monday morning, she would wake early, drag herself to the subway, then walk five blocks to Powell-Standish. She'd have to face her cramped office and Bradley's smug grin, a Merit likely dangling from his lips.

Then what? Bradley's Adidas crushing her fingers as he scrambled past her on his way up the corporate ladder? Her life had been reduced to a depressing, menacing cartoon.

How the hell did she get here? Within the confines of her rental Toyota, Kit let out a bloodcurdling scream, the release cathartic. She coughed out a laugh. What the fuck was she supposed to do now? Kit knew what Jonathan Wakefield would have advised in a rife moment like this.

Write about it.

Where had that come from? She hadn't thought about her former English professor lately. Considering all the people she'd known in her life, few had left a lasting impression. Jonathan Wakefield was certainly one of them. His encouragement had given her the confidence to pursue writing, his recommendation landing her the scholarship at NYU, changing the entire course of her life. He'd given her a shot, and for that, she owed the man a debt of gratitude.

When Kit split for New York, Jonathan made changes of his own. If memory served, he'd moved to San Francisco. Could he still be here?

Kit bolted away. Away from the airport, her flight, her apartment, her job—her entire life. As if self-propelled, the rental car ferried her across an ocean of roiling city traffic until she reached the southern end of Golden Gate Park. When she spotted a parking place, she accidentally jerked to a stop, stalling the engine in the dead middle of the lane. Horns beeped intermittently, then insistently. Unlike New Yorkers, Californians were obsessed with living in their damn cars. Why didn't anybody take transit or walk, for shit's sake? Checking the rearview, she confirmed the crush closing in behind her. Kit managed to grind the motor to a start. She yanked the steering wheel hard, backing falteringly toward the parking spot, when her bumper scraped excruciatingly against a signpost.

As cars streamed by, she sat frozen in the driver's seat, aware of her hands clutching the steering wheel, the sound of her own shallow breathing. As if awakening from deep sleep, reality sank in. She dabbed at her eyes with her shirtsleeve. What the fucking hell was she doing here? And why couldn't she stop crying? She'd clearly gone off the rails. For starters, she'd failed to return the rental car. More critically, she'd missed her flight and would not be clocking in Monday morning. The girl who'd never cut classes, never skipped a day of work, had fallen off the face of the earth. Kit had never been a rule breaker, but now she'd deliberately sabotaged her schedule.

Katherine Hilliard—AWOL. It had a certain ring to it.

She steered into a proper spot and set the parking brake. With nothing left to lose, the future beckoned, open-ended and luminous. Feeling a little reckless and free to do as she pleased, Kit grabbed her jacket and set out on foot. On pure instinct, she tramped into the woods, picking up her pace as if she could outrun her fears. The biting scent of eucalyptus evoked a distant, faded memory then the image sharpened.

She still recalled the fall day in 1971, the endless drive north. Kit had been both scared and thrilled to leave home for the first time. She was going to college, which for her meant hallowed ground, the fulfillment of her deepest desire. All the way to Humboldt she'd counted the miles that would separate her from her dad.

Before that day, Kit had rarely ventured from her hometown, a desert wasteland on the outskirts of nowhere. She remembered now. Her dad had parked the old Buick not far from here so they could stretch their legs in Golden Gate Park. San Francisco's chill air, wet with fog, had seemed otherworldly then. As she and her dad strolled through the park, the discovery of an intimate Japanese tea garden hidden in the heart of the pulsating city underscored the boundless world, all the unknown places beyond San Bernardino County.

Kit hadn't thought about that auspicious day in ages, but now, as she plodded down the trail, images rushed in. She recalled the slatted park bench, sitting alongside her dad in awkward silence. As she'd chewed her peanut butter sandwich and sipped her warm Coke, emotions rocked around in her head. Bound for Arcata to begin her first semester at Humboldt, her whole body had tingled with anticipation. At the same time, when she studied her father's unreadable expression, her heart ached with knowing. She was moving away from him, and there would be no turning back.

She savored the long-lost memory of her seventeen-year-old self, wishing she could hold onto it. If only she could summon such memories at will, to conjure her sense of wonder, to feel her body, electrified, stepping into the unknown. Kit shoved her hands deep in her coat pockets and plodded onward. Head bent; she concentrated on the hypnotic movement of her impractically high heels on the uneven ground. The sharp stems of her pumps speared the eucalyptus leaves blanketed below, as a vaguely medicinal odor drifted up and seeped into her consciousness.

She is seven, sick all week with a deep, raspy cough. Her father's face is taut with concentration. He digs into the blue jar of VapoRub, his calloused hands clumsily applying the ointment to her chest. He kisses her forehead and tells her goodnight. After he is gone, she is alone in the dark and she is scared. She wonders, but does not ask, when her mother will come home.

The tightness in her chest stopped her in her tracks.

Kit broke through the woods into the gray light, finding herself on a deserted asphalt road. Remnants of the past still hung in the air as she scanned her surroundings. She looked heavenward, hoping to find clarity, but thick churning clouds obscured her vision. Raindrops began to dribble, then spat angrily at the ground. A lump of self-pity lodged in her throat. She needed a hero, a voice of reason—she needed her father. Her lower lip trembled, but she refused to cry. She planted her feet and steeled herself—she was a New Yorker now, for Christ's sake. She'd been in worse scrapes. Hedging her bets, she walked along the wet road and in no time spotted signs of civilization. Kit instantly recognized the iconic architecture of the Conservatory of Flowers, as familiar as running into an old friend.

She'd often stopped near the elegant greenhouse on her way to and from Humboldt. With a distant gaze, she half smiled, recalling those days—perhaps the best days of her life. If only she could turn back the clock. Kit acknowledged that time travel was not an option, and she recognized her tendency to view her college years through the rose-colored lens of hindsight. But still, she had to admit, those were heady days—overwrought with angst, passion, and creativity. A wave of gloom washed over her. When had she lost that spark and where exactly had it gone? Swallowed up by the mean streets?

Maybe. But maybe she'd simply grown up. Kit acknowledged her advantages. She had a decent job, one many people would kill for. Her East Village walk-up, another "kill for" coup. The rain let up, leaving a sweetness in the air. Kit inhaled deeply to clear her head. She considered the obvious, sensible path. She'd simply cut her losses, hightail it back to the airport, and salvage her life. Today had only been a hiccup, a flight of fancy. This was fixable.

Kit backtracked to the rental car, taking inventory. The back bumper bore an ugly scar, and when she tried to start it up, the engine wouldn't budge. In matters of dead cars, her father had trained her well—walk briskly to the nearest call box and summon AAA. After making contact, she prepared to wait for an eternity. To her surprise, a bright-yellow tow truck lumbered up minutes later. The driver jumped out, yanked open the passenger door, and gestured for Kit to get in. She grabbed her suitcase, tossed it into the musty cab, and hoisted herself aboard.

33

The man nimbly hitched up the rental, wiped his hands on his pants, and climbed in next to her. He looked to be in his mid-forties and smelled of tobacco, bourbon, and breath mints. His hands were grease-stained, his beard unkempt, but his eyes were kind. Kit judged him *safe*.

He turned to her. "Looks like you flooded it." He pondered for a moment. "Might be an alternator."

Kit shifted in her seat. "Is that expensive?"

He revved the engine. "Depends," he said. "Which shop are you using?"

She pictured the scraped bumper, her mind racing. She considered returning the car to Hertz, but having declined the optional insurance, she feared she'd be liable for any damages. Wouldn't they gouge her? The thought of burning through her savings for some stupid car repair sickened her. She'd worked hard for that money.

The man inched the truck forward. "So, where are we going?"

"Well, I'm not exactly sure. I don't live around here." Her temples began to throb. "Here's my auto club card," she said as she handed it to him.

He glanced at the card and handed it back. "Yeah, that's just for the tow."

Fuck. Could this day get any crazier? Even if she'd wanted to, she couldn't call her dad. He didn't need the added pressure on his heart. And how would she explain her actions? *By the way, I ran away, ditched my flight and thrashed the rental car.*

"I don't really have a lot of money," she blurted.

Drawing a pack of Marlboro's from his shirt pocket, he shook one loose, sparked a match and lit up. He took a drag and the cab filled with smoke. "I know a guy who might fix it on the cheap."

A plan fell into place. She would call Hertz to extend her rental contract for an extra day or two. She'd get the bumper repaired and they'd never know the difference. "Sounds good."

The driver unhitched the car, giving her a nod as he drove away. She paused for moment, glancing up at the orange Shell logo, and took in the noisy, bustling intersection with the bus stop across the street with its shrine to John Lennon. Apparently today *could* get crazier. Déjà fucking vu.

She entered the dank garage, same as she had a week ago, but didn't see the attendant. "Hello?" she called boldly. When she heard no reply, she peeped into the adjacent office and found Ben behind the counter.

He glanced up and grinned, like he'd been expecting her. "You're back."

Kit noted the countertop cluttered with books, paperwork, and spent Pepsi bottles. "I'm in a bit of a jam," she began, all the while wondering how she'd previously overlooked his deep brown eyes and warm smile. She went on to explain her predicament.

Ben cocked his head as if thinking it over. "Look, I can get a salvaged bumper and fix it up for you. You'll owe me for the part, but I won't charge you for labor. It might take a couple days. I'll have to work on it between the paying jobs."

"A couple of days?" Where on earth would she go?

"Yep. Give or take."

Fresh out of options, Kit agreed. She was stuck. Apart from all reason, the open-ended, possibly catastrophic future didn't faze her. Perhaps fate had beckoned her here, to this unique place and time, for a purpose not yet evident. On that note, she made a bargain with the universe. If Jonathan's number happened to be listed, she'd take it as a sign. "Can I use your phone?"

Ben pointed to a black wall phone. "Knock yourself out."

A customer pulled up to the full-service pump and Ben hustled outside.

Kit spotted the phonebook on the counter. She picked it up, weighing its bulk. It'd seen better days, she thought, thumbing its tattered, grease-blackened, dog-eared pages. When she got to the W section, she braced for the coin toss. She ran her finger down the page, and sure enough, *Wakefield, Jonathan* jumped out. No initials, no guessing—no doubt.

That Same Day
San Francisco

Jonathan savored the peace and quiet as Dylan slept.

"Pop?"

So much for quiet. The sight of the boy's cowlick sticking out at a comical angle, his rumpled dinosaur pajamas, too small for him now, made Jonathan chuckle. A cub emerging from winter's hibernation. "Good morning, buddy."

Dylan yawned and rubbed his eyes, then crawled onto Jonathan's lap. "Dad?"

"Yes?"

"Can we make chicken piccata? With rice and broccoli?"

Jonathan creased his newspaper and set it on the table. He smoothed his boy's hair, taking in his familiar sleep scent, feral and slightly gamey. "You know, kiddo, it's a little early for dinner."

Dylan moaned. "I know, Dad. But we'll have to walk to the market," he reasoned. "We're out of olive oil and capers."

His son's slight build and youthful rosy cheeks belied his mature intellect. The kid was ten going on forty. Jonathan had to admire his tenacity. "You do make a valid point."

"I think we might need lemons, too."

Under Jonathan's tutelage, Dylan had become a culinary enthusiast. He especially loved baking, transforming raw ingredients—sugar, flour, milk, and butter—into an entirely different entity. His specialty: peanut butter chocolate chip brownies.

Dylan huddled in closer, his hot breath millimeters from his dad's ear. "So, when do we go?"

Jonathan took a sip of his coffee, now tepid. "Tell you what, we'll go just as soon as I finish reading the paper."

"That will take infinity," Dylan groaned.

"No, only a fraction of infinity."

Dylan headed for the kitchen and returned with a bowl of Cheerios. Resigned, he flopped down on the couch and opened his tattered copy of *Chronicles of Narnia*, settling in for the duration.

They continued reading in companionable silence as they often did on lazy Sunday mornings. Jonathan cherished these mornings, more so since Dylan had moved in with Kara and Kent. With Dylan relegated to weekend visits, he tried to make the most of their limited time together. He realized he spoiled Dylan a bit. Guilty as charged, but not the worst crime, he supposed.

Glancing at his son curled up with a book, Jonathan's heart swelled. It hadn't been a straight line, but he and Kara had done okay. A feeling of peace washed over him. His son was thriving. Jonathan's last novel still paid the bills. Milo had come back to him, his romantic life taking an unexpected turn for the better. Searching his heart, he found nothing lacking. That is, nothing he could name.

His thoughts were broken by the ringing phone—no doubt Milo, checking in, their weekend routine now well ingrained. On Fridays and Saturdays, his time belonged to Dylan. Milo joined them for dinner on Sunday evenings. After Kara picked Dylan up, Milo stayed over.

"I got it," Dylan sang as he bolted from the couch to the kitchen. A moment later, the child called out, "Da-a-d, it's for you."

"Who is it?" Jonathan called.

Dylan wandered back into the living room and picked up his book.

Jonathan rose from his chair. "Hey, kiddo. Is it Milo?"

Dylan shrugged. "Nah, it's just some lady."

"Did she mention her name?"

He yawned and shrugged. "I think, maybe Katherine?"

Jonathan's heart raced. *Katherine.* The name conjured the visage of a youthful, startlingly intelligent woman. He hurried into the kitchen to find the receiver dangling in midair. When would Dylan learn to use the telephone stand? "Katherine?" he said. "Is it you?"

"It's me."

While other pupils had long since blurred into the ether, Katherine's light still shone. In truth, he liked to think he'd played some small role in molding this exceptional human. "What a nice surprise."

"I hope I haven't caught you at a bad time."

Her voice conjured a trunkful of emotions, a potpourri of baggage. In the big picture, his year in Humboldt County had been an interlude, fraught, to say the least. There, he'd sunk to new lows, crawled and scratched his way out. "No, not at all. I'm delighted you called. It's wonderful to hear your voice."

"Good to hear yours, too."

Sifting through memories, he couldn't recall the last time they'd spoken. He poured himself another cup and pulled up a chair, settling in for a long-overdue catch-up session. "My God, how long has it been?"

"A few years, that's for sure."

"Wasn't it at your book signing?"

"I think you're right," she said.

He'd been in New York on business when he decided to dip into the tiny Greenwich bookshop and surprise Katherine. Recalling the sparse audience, which had included Zelda and Katherine's father, he'd sympathized with Katherine. In the beginning, he too, had endured many readings with marginal turnouts. "Time certainly flies."

"It sure does."

He pictured the quiet girl in the back row. The girl with untidy hair, diminutive frame, too-big backpack slung over her bird-like shoulder, hovering outside his office door, too shy to knock. An innocent; a lost lamb. The passage of time notwithstanding, this impression of her stuck in his mind like an old photograph, unchanging. "Tell me about your life, Katherine. How have you been?"

"Good."

Jonathan sensed her hesitation but plowed ahead anyway. "How's New York? Are you still loving it?"

A long moment of silence ensued as if Katherine's verbal well had run dry. "It's fine," she hedged.

Then it hit him. When Zelda sold the Greene Agency, he may have lost a damn good agent, but Katherine had lost her job. He'd heard she'd been picked up by Powell-Standish, best known for cash cow celebrity clients. With a twinge of guilt, he ventured forth. "And Powell-Standish? How's that going?"

"Frankly, it's kind of mind-numbing."

"Sorry," he said.

Katherine said nothing.

He heard her sniff, as if holding back tears. The girl never could hide her heart. "Katherine, are you okay?"

"Not really," she managed.

"Do you want to talk about it?"

She released ragged breath. "My dad recently had a heart attack."

"Jesus, is he okay?"

"Yes, he's okay. Still healing, but he's going to be fine."

Jonathan straightened his spine, his chest puffing with paternal protection. "Shit. Sounds like you've had a pretty rough go, kid. How can I help?"

She chuckled ruefully. "Well, I could use a favor."

"Anything," he said without hesitation.

Jonathan fumbled with his shirt, buttoning and unbuttoning until he got it right. He rallied Dylan and they scrambled down the narrow staircase into the tiny basement garage. "Hop in the back seat," he instructed, patting the boy's back.

"Why do I have to sit back there?"

"My old friend is in town. I thought she might like to sit up front with me," he bargained.

Dylan shrugged sulkily. "Can I sit up front then move when we get her?"

Jonathan smirked. Not a fight-worthy battle. "Yes, okay," he conceded.

He backed down the tight driveway onto the street and turned to Dylan, who was still wearing his too-small pajama top with jeans and sneakers. "Buckle up."

Dylan dragged the seatbelt over his shoulder and secured it with a click. "Where's your friend?"

"Her car broke down. She's at a repair shop."

He nodded. "How do you know her?"

"She used to be my student."

"How old is she?"

"I don't know. Late twenties."

Dylan's curiosity momentarily appeased; Jonathan focused on driving. Sunday's light traffic made the journey from Cole Valley brief. Within moments, he spied a diminutive woman on the sidewalk, suitcase in hand. He recognized Katherine, but she'd visibly changed. No longer a girl, but a woman. Her air more sophisticated, her clothing refined, hairstyle polished. If they'd bumped into each other on some arbitrary street, he doubted he would have known her.

He made a U-turn, pulled into the Shell Station and hopped out to greet her.

"Jonathan," she called, her face lighting up.

He wrapped his arms around her. She collapsed into him; her head pressed to his breastbone. He stroked her hair, as he would a child's, breathing in the scent of strawberry shampoo. Overcome with emotion, he felt as if his heart might crack open. And in that exquisite moment, the world made perfect sense. His little lamb had returned.

That Very Same Day, continued
San Francisco

Kit stepped out of the overheated Volvo into the damp San Francisco chill and ascended a steep concrete staircase to Jonathan's apartment. Immediately struck by the relative quiet inside, she realized the solid plaster walls and leaded glass windows muted the street noises below. Her gaze traveled from the grand ceiling down to the polished hardwood floors. The little touches, such as decorative wainscoting and light fixtures, whether modern-day reproductions or lovingly restored Victorian-era décor, managed to convey formality as well as warmth. By comparison, her cramped New York walk-up was a hovel. "Your place is so nice," she said, dumbly stating the obvious.

Jonathan gave her a sheepish smile. "Thanks," he said. "It's a work in progress."

Dylan rocked back and forth on his heels. He paused as if preparing to speak. "Katherine, do you like chicken piccata?" he asked, his voice timorous.

She took a long look at the boy. With his slight build, dark hair, big brown eyes, and flawless skin, the word *pretty* sprang to mind. "Actually, it's my favorite."

Dylan grinned at her, revealing a neat row of transparent braces on his upper teeth. "Mine, too," he said.

Kit wondered if the braces might explain his shy manner.

41

Dylan looked to his father. "Is she staying for dinner?"

Jonathan gave Kit a knowing grin. "She'd better."

Kit turned to Dylan. "I'd love to stay."

The boy's rosy cheeks reddened a shade. "Don't forget, Dad. We still need lemons and olive oil."

"I haven't forgotten," Jonathan said. "After I visit with Katherine for a while, maybe we'll walk down to the market." He glanced at the boy's pajama top. "You're going to need a clean shirt."

Dylan stole a furtive glance at Kit, turned on his heels, and disappeared, presumably to his bedroom.

"Terrific kid," Kit said once he was out of earshot.

"He is pretty terrific," Jonathan agreed, his pride unhidden.

She trailed behind him through the living room and down the hallway, where he pointed out Dylan's room to the right, his large master bedroom to the left. Entering the bright kitchen, Kit noted the vintage stove, beveled glass cabinets and cozy breakfast nook, the walls and high ceilings painted creamy white. Again, she stated the obvious. "Great kitchen."

"Thanks. It's the main reason I wanted this apartment."

She nodded as she contemplated Jonathan's still-handsome face. Among the unwashed throng in Humboldt County, he'd certainly stood out as a smart dresser—hence the sophomoric nickname "Necktie." But now, he looked different. Still drop-dead gorgeous, but his dark hair was cropped closer, bringing out his dreamy brown eyes. Kit struggled to avoid ogling the cut of his snug Levi's and his chiseled biceps when it finally registered. Jonathan no longer portrayed the role of a stereotypical straight guy. His move to the city had set him free. Her former prof had come out—as himself—and she approved of the change.

He placed a palm on her shoulder. "I'll bet you're exhausted after the morning you've had."

Even if she'd wanted to, she couldn't hide. He'd always seen right through her. "I am a little tired," she conceded.

"Let's get you settled," he said, tugging hard on the back door until it sprang open. "After you."

Kit's curiosity piqued. "There's more?"

"Follow me," he said, leading her into a tiny private backyard.

The sun had come out and it blinded her momentarily. They walked past a small patch of overgrown grass, a brick patio with wrought iron table and chairs. Circling around the back of the house, they arrived at an outbuilding.

"Welcome to our guest room," he said, jiggling the crystal knob. "I suppose I should say guest room and summer writing studio." He yanked hard on the door. "Every door in the house is stuck, swollen from the rain."

Kit hung on the threshold, staring at her shoes. Was she imposing? After all, they weren't exactly friends, more like mentor and mentee. Perhaps he didn't have the heart to turn her away. Worry tugged at her heartstrings.

He held the door open for her and she stepped inside. If he'd noticed her hesitance, he didn't mention it. "This little cottage used to be the maid's quarters, or so I'm told. I'm afraid it's pretty bare bones. There's no heat out here, but I can bring in a portable if you need it."

She took a breath. "Don't bother with the heater; I'm sure it'll be fine. I'm used to icy winters."

He gave her a sideways look then shrugged. "Okay, let me know if you change your mind."

"Really, this is so kind of you. I'm sure the car will be ready in a day or so." In truth, she had no idea. "Jonathan?"

"Yes?"

"I can't thank you enough."

He studied her. "You're welcome. My house is yours, however long you may need it." He smiled, the lines around his eyes crinkling. "I'll put on a pot of coffee. After you settle in, come on back to the main house so we can catch up."

Jonathan's generosity touched her, making her eyes well up, but she managed to hold it together—barely.

"By the way, I have news."

She couldn't begin to imagine what he might want to tell her, but the glint in his eye hinted it would be good, perhaps another novel in the pipeline. "Okay, I'll be in soon."

"I'll leave you to it, then."

Once he was gone, Kit appraised her compact quarters. He'd thought of everything: comfy chair and reading lamp by the window, bed with lofty down comforter, small writing desk. Peeking into the bathroom, she discovered the old-fashioned black-and-white honeycomb tile flooring, the narrow window above the big claw-foot tub. All of it fitting, somehow, in keeping with her image of Jonathan. She opened the closest, tidy and cedar-scented, then reached for a hanger. Her weighty woolen coat reminded her of snow, the New York winter she'd left behind.

Kit sat down on the bed, her slightest movement issuing wheezy squeaks from the bedsprings. She bounced a little, smiling and relishing this tiny imperfection in Jonathan's otherwise flawless aesthetic. Glancing at her watch, she found it frozen at eight fifteen. She held it to her ear and listened for ticking, pronounced it dead, and placed it on the nightstand. Talk about a time warp. This morning, sipping orange juice at her dad's kitchen table in Pacifica, she'd been New York bound. Now she found herself in this gem of a cottage. It was like some clever trickery she couldn't quite wrap her mind around.

In a matter of hours, Kit's buttoned-down life had loosened, her will bending to the absolute randomness of the universe. While she acknowledged the inevitability of tomorrow, for today time stood still. Visions of her one-and-only love, Joe, came to mind unbidden, bringing heat to her cheeks. Perhaps fate had called her back to California — to him. A second wind filling her lungs, she washed her face, brushed her hair, and changed into her comfiest jeans.

Kit strolled with father and son to the nearby corner market, gleaning lemons, capers, and olive oil for dinner, chocolate chip ice cream for dessert. For the balance of the day, she chatted with Jonathan in his sunny breakfast nook while Dylan busied himself in his bedroom. Sipping coffee and chewing on safe topics, such as weather and politics, they skirted around the unspoken elephant in the room. But eventually, as she knew he would, he gently prodded her.

"How's the writing?" he asked, his tone breezy.

"I seem to have hit a bit of a wall," she said, grossly understating it. She didn't mention the gnawing dread in her gut, debilitating her, tying her hands.

"It happens to everyone." He looked at her pointedly. "That is, everyone who's any good."

She no longer considered herself *good*, but as a one-shot wonder—an imposter. Her confidence had been shaken, her momentum lost, and somewhere along the line, she'd simply given up.

His eyes bored into her as if he could read her mind. "Look, I know your book didn't get much traction, but that's no reason to quit."

She hadn't thought about her book in years, and now it evoked the memory of Lester Cap, whose sudden death had left her shaken. Former mailman, hybrid rhododendron breeder, genius and all-around character, Lester had once been a grandfather figure to Kit, and the inspiration for her briefly celebrated volume. Kit never got a chance to thank him, to say goodbye, and to this day carried her regret like a block of cement.

Jonathan wore a faraway look. "Sometimes it's good to shake things up."

Kit nodded but wished he'd quit trying to mentor her; she was not his student, after all. Her book may have tanked, her writing stalled, but she'd made peace with it—the past was *in the past*. She disliked digging up old skeletons.

He pressed on. "I'm sorry about Zelda shutting down Greene. That must have been brutal, but you landed on your feet, Katherine, and I commend you." He hesitated. "I don't think Powell-Standish is the right place for you, though. I'm afraid it's a dead end."

Kit swallowed the lump in her throat. "Well, I don't disagree with you," she hedged. "But a job's a job."

Jonathan said nothing. He didn't have to. His face said it all.

She felt like his pupil again, tongue-tied, uncertain of the "right" answer. Her cheeks heated up. "I need to work; I need to pay the bills."

He studied her. "You need to write."

Jonathan didn't get it. His writing generated income. He lived in a perfect apartment in a perfect city with a perfect son. "I don't have time to focus on writing. I'm really busy," she said.

He wore the expression of a disappointed elder. "Katherine, I expected something more original. Busy? A little timeworn, as excuses go."

"It's not that simple."

Jonathan shrugged. "Well, if you want a place to focus, I'm not using the studio. It's yours if you want it."

Before Kit could formulate a response, Dylan showed up. Jonathan's attention transferred to him, changing the very air in the room.

The boy wore a sheepish expression. "Poppy, isn't it time for dinner?"

Jonathan rose from his seat. "You're right, kiddo. We'd better rally the troops."

Kit was grateful for the interruption, happy for the subject of her writing to be tabled. With any luck, Jonathan would let it drop. As afternoon dissolved into evening, she took pleasure in ordinary rituals. Slicing tomatoes and peeling carrots, she belonged to the human family again, her feet planted on the earth. Dylan kept a watchful eye on the stove, where a pot of rice bubbled and thin chicken breasts, fragrant with lemons and garlic, sautéed. Glancing at Jonathan, busy whisking salad dressing, she recalled his earlier words. "Jonathan?"

He turned to her. "Yes?"

"I almost forgot. You were going to share some news?"

He gave her a sparkling grin. "Yes, but I decided to surprise you instead."

She set her knife on the cutting board. What on earth? "A surprise? I'm intrigued."

A knock at the kitchen door sent a shiver up her spine. She turned to witness the doorknob jiggling, the door swinging wide open. The caller whirled in like a dervish, and for a split second she didn't recognize him.

A tall, angular, curly-headed man stood before her eyes, a loaf of French bread in one hand, a bunch of purple delphiniums in the other. "Hey, Kit-Kat," he said with nonchalance.

Kit took in a sharp breath, doubting her own eyes. "Milo?"

Milo set the bread and flowers down on the counter. "Present," he said with that trademark grin of his. Then he swept her into his arms.

San Francisco
The Day After Katherine's Arrival

Jonathan's recent bout with insomnia perplexed him as he couldn't pinpoint any specific cause.

He found himself constantly awake at two or three in the morning, alert. For the most part, it didn't bother him. He'd switch on his light to read or write, suffering no ill effects the next day.

But today he woke before six with brain fuzz, the buildup of many sleepless nights dulling his wits. Dragging his bones out of bed, he yawned, lifted the window shade, and glanced across the street.

A little red Datsun backed haltingly over the curb. It bumped, scraped, lurched forward, then died. He recognized the driver as his reclusive neighbor, a humorless woman of indeterminate years. The first time he encountered her in passing, he'd tried making eye contact, but she'd plowed ahead as if she couldn't be bothered to acknowledge his existence. Unfazed, Jonathan attempted neighborly greetings, friendly waves and smiles, but she invariably snubbed him. Her wordless rebuffs, for reasons he didn't understand, amplified his curiosity. The woman was an enigma and he wanted to crack the code. Getting the grump to engage became his secret pet project.

He'd discovered her occupation, toll taker on the Golden Gate Bridge, by accident. After a weekend party up at the Russian River, he'd pulled up to her booth and handed her his buck. He'd recognized her right away and gave her an effusive *hello*. Her expression flatlined before she turned away. Jonathan knew when to quit. He lost his desire to know her and eventually she fell off his radar altogether.

Until now. Studying her as he would an anthropology subject or perhaps an animal in its habitat, he contemplated her as she rolled down her car window and tossed a smoldering cigarette to the street. She revved the engine and made her way off the curb. Jonathan tracked the little car as it chugged into the mist, taillights fading into nothingness. In that moment, the old melancholy washed over him, the leaden sadness he carried never fully at bay. How easy it would be to succumb, to flump back to bed.

But he knew better. Jonathan had traveled that road headfirst into the abyss, and nothing good had ever come of it. He steeled himself, calling up his timeworn motto, *brew a pot of joe and get the day rolling—one foot in front of the other*. Though not especially creative or original, it had served him well.

On his way to the kitchen, he paused at Dylan's bedroom, vacant for the duration of the school week. In the boy's absence, the room took on a stillness, as if holding its breath until Dylan returned. Jonathan stripped the bed, gathered books and stray socks from the floor. He placed the books on the shelf, stuffed the sheets into the wicker hamper, and advanced to the utility porch. As he engaged the dials, the hum of the washer reassured him, the cycle in motion. Today, he knew, would be too quiet. But on Friday, he'd pick Dylan up after school. There would be clean clothes, fresh cotton sheets, and noise.

Scents of toasting bread and strong java brightened Jonathan's mood. Gathering his notes for that evening's graduate seminar, he settled in at the kitchen table. A tap at the kitchen door startled him. He'd been so caught up in his head, he'd completely forgotten his house guest. "Come in," he called.

Katherine wrestled the door open, bringing a gust of cold air. "Good morning, Jonathan."

She seemed in good spirits, well rested. "You're up early," he said.

She'd swept her curls into a high twisted bun, leaving her slender neck exposed. He found the hairstyle becoming. He added two slices of bread to the toaster. "How did you sleep?" he asked.

"Like a ton of bricks." She let out a chuckle. "That room is so peaceful."

He nodded. "Good."

Katherine slid into the breakfast nook, returning to her original spot as if to resume yesterday's conversation.

"Breakfast?" Jonathan asked.

"I'd love some," she said.

Jonathan poured her a cup. He buttered two slices of toast, cut them into triangles, and arranged them on a turquoise Fiesta plate.

"Thanks," she said. "Looks delicious." Reaching for the pot of orange marmalade, she suppressed a grin.

"What's so amusing?"

"I was thinking about Waffle Hamlet." She smiled at some distant memory. "Those were crazy times."

He envisioned the first time he'd encountered young Katherine, the reserved waitress who later showed up in his senior seminar at Humboldt. "What made you go there?"

She pointed to the marmalade. "Milo used to call it mucus," she said, coughing out a laugh.

"Ah, the very soul of wit," Jonathan said. He recalled the two of them, thick as thieves, clear as if it were yesterday. Lanky Milo, the frenetic jester. Petite, earnest Katherine, the grounding force. And there had been a third one, Erin, Katherine's ersatz friend and classmate who'd gone off the rails. Parenthetically, he wondered whatever became of her. "You two were quite a pair."

She wore a faraway look. "Yeah. Milo made that job tolerable, always cracking me up."

He considered how far she had come since her Waffle Hamlet days. He'd been thrilled for her when she graduated from NYU. Her collection of short stories had been accepted by a minor publisher, and she'd accepted the job at Greene. Her future looked luminous, her path set. But now, he feared, she'd lost her way. "Katherine, my offer still stands. The studio is yours if you want it. Your own personal writer's retreat—rent free. Have you thought about it?"

She avoided his eyes. "I have."

"But?"

"But it's a little overwhelming. I can't just drop everything."

"I can talk to Robert, if you'd like me too. I'm sure I could persuade him to offer you leave of absence from your job." As he said it, he wondered if he still had the clout.

Her eyes widened. "You know Robert Powell?"

He remembered Rob, Powell-Standish's founder, from the early days. Rob began his career working for Zelda at Greene. A young, brash upstart, circling the water—a shark. Jonathan never much cared for Rob, but the man owed him a favor. "We've met."

Katherine appeared contemplative, her face unreadable. "Small world," she said.

The air in the room thickened. He reached across the table and touched her hand. "Have I upset you?"

She picked up her mug and set it down again. "Just the opposite. You've made me incredibly happy." Katherine met his eyes. "I'm so grateful for all your help, Jonathan. And I promise I will think about what you said. But before I can make any major decisions, I need to deal with my mess."

"Ah, yes. Would you like a ride to the body shop?"

She glanced at her watch, then her eyes sparked. "Actually, Milo's picking me up—right now."

Jonathan's thoughts traveled to last night. Gathered around the dinner table with old friends, he'd savored the sublime company. He'd relished Dylan's chicken down to the last caper, the last drop of lemony sauce. Milo and Katherine's reunion had touched him. From a strictly objective standpoint, he couldn't imagine a more blissful evening. Why, then, did shameful little nails of jealousy still scratch at him?

As they'd finished breakfast, Milo swept in to whisk Katherine away. Jonathan returned to his lecture notes sans distractions. He welcomed his solitude and the quiet he needed to think, but on reflection, admittedly, he felt a little left out. He couldn't figure out why it bothered him, if he were jealous of Milo or Katherine—or both? Clearly, neither scenario had any basis in logic.

He understood that the two of them shared an exceptional bond, but their friendship didn't diminish their connection to him. Or did it?

The Next Day
San Francisco

Climbing aboard Milo's vintage VW van, Kit was immediately transported to her senior year at Humboldt, a fond remembrance of her own beloved minibus. Milo's van, of the same late 1960s vintage, smelled faintly of worn vinyl like Kit's, but the resemblance ended there. His entire camper had been gutted and sculpted into a pickup truck only hipper and more stylish. She envisioned him wielding a giant blowtorch, carving out this one-of-a-kind custom vehicle. "Cool car," she said. "Did you do it yourself?"

"No, my cousin Landreth did the conversion. Sold it to me for five hundred bucks."

Milo's unending ancestral roster, a colorful bunch of cousins, aunts, uncles, and grandparents, never ceased to flummox Kit. "I'd say you got a good deal."

He shifted into second. "Yeah."

Milo's mythic extended family had continuously bestowed blessings— fresh-caught salmon, truckloads of scrap metal, a free rental house. The thought of Milo's close-knit familial network brought a vague sensation of loss. She recalled Milo's fond stories about working alongside his grandpa George, a native Hoopa salmon fisherman. Kit adored her father and wouldn't trade places even if she could. Still, she couldn't help but wonder what she might be missing. She imagined that Milo's abundant relatives, as well as connection to the Native American culture, had provided him a feeling of belonging she'd never know.

"I needed a truck to haul some of my heavier pieces," he said. He rode the clutch, then bullied it into gear, chugging up a steep hill.

Kit took in the impossible vertical incline of the road. Everything was happening so fast, her surroundings so foreign, so new. One thing was certain—she wasn't in New York anymore. "So, when do I get to see your stuff?"

The van struggled up the hill then idled at a red light. Milo glanced over at Kit. His eyes brightened. "First things first, missy. After we deal with your rental car shit, we can stop by the gallery."

"Sounds reasonable."

When she thought about Milo's art, she envisioned his place in Samoa, a lonely sandspit off Humboldt Bay. Amid the thick fog and scents of salt and rotting seaweed, a jumble of ever-changing whimsical sculptures inhabited in his front yard. Intricate dragons, giant Dungeness crabs, clunky vintage cars—whatever—sinking into shifting sand. Milo would often disappear for weeks at a time, driven to bring his quirky vision to life. He tinkered with found objects: driftwood, scrap metal, anything he could get his hands on. Then he might go months between projects, as if building momentum, waiting for inspiration to strike. Kit admired his passion and talent. His work was extraordinary. But deep down, she'd wished he would quit screwing around, get serious, and go to college.

Who knew Milo's art would be discovered by a Berlin art dealer driving by his place on some Northern California sight-seeing tour? In the mid-seventies, shortly after Kit set out for NYU, she'd been sipping hot chocolate in the student union when she stumbled upon the *Times* article: "European Collectors Hunger for Outsider Art." When she'd discovered Milo's face among the featured artists, she'd practically fallen off her chair. With no formal training, he'd ascended the ranks, instantly in demand, a working artist—no small feat. That night, they'd blabbed on the phone for hours. But in the following months, he'd faded from her life. She'd subsisted on an occasional postcard from his travels, then nothing.

Then Milo informed her of the wildest twist: Jonathan's ex-wife, Kara had led him straight to Jonathan's door. Kit glanced at her dear friend and felt the years between them dissolve. Despite her decidedly shitty life, she couldn't stop smiling. "I've missed the hell out of you," she said.

He flashed her that dazzling grin. "Me, too," Milo said. He let out a laugh.

"What's so funny?"

"This cassette. It reminds me of our dance parties."

Kit's memories about her Waffle Hamlet days had receded into black and white, shapeless and blurry. But in Milo's company, they flooded back in full color. Blasting music, singing off-key at the top of their lungs, dancing around like maniacs, all the while vacuuming, loading the dishwasher, or cleaning out the disgusting fryer. Four tedious years at the greasy spoon would have been pure drudgery, but Milo's mischief made the hours fly. He never failed to shake things up. She'd be taking an order all somber and serious-faced and he'd try to distract her, tossing bits of food at her feet or making goofy faces. Or he'd snatch uneaten pancakes from people's plates and hide them throughout the restaurant like Easter eggs. She'd find them in the funniest places, like her own shoes or coat pockets. His antics often made her double over, laughing so hard she nearly peed her pants. She grinned remembering. "Those were crazy times."

He patted her shoulder. "Crazy good."

She gave him an exaggerated wink. "Especially after-hours."

On rare occasions, post-movie or after parties, they'd slip into Waffle Hamlet for an illicit late-night binge. Under ghostly fluorescent kitchen lighting, they'd down stacks of pancakes topped with vanilla ice cream, smothered in blackberry syrup. Recalling those uncomplicated times, her chest tightened. Their friendship had been a fluke. She'd never met anyone like Milo, before or since. His clown-like personality may have drawn her in, but his kind heart had won her abiding affection. "It's weird, but I almost miss it," she said.

"Yeah, me, too. Those were the days, old chum." He changed the tape, then the subject. "But hey. How about right now?" he said, shaking his head. "Talk about crazy times, right?"

"What do you mean?"

"For starters, the two of us landing in San Francisco. I can't believe you just showed up at Jon's."

Kit had to concede the point. Reconnecting first with Jonathan, then Milo, bore the earmarks of divine intervention. She felt her life changing, moving in fast-forward. And it felt exhilarating. For once in her cautious, resistant life, she'd jumped into the water, allowing the wave to take her. "Yeah, it's pretty random."

His gaze fixed on some invisible horizon. "The stars have aligned."

"Speaking of stars lining up, do I detect a serious romance?"

Milo's face gave nothing away. "Perhaps," he hedged.

Kit folded her arms across her chest. "Listen, mister. You need to spill it. What's going on between you and Jonathan? Are you, like, an item?"

His spine straightened. "We've been seeing each other for a while now, taking it slow."

Taking it slow had never been in Milo's wheelhouse. Clearly time had mellowed him. "Is that your idea or his?"

He drew breath. "I think we're both a little wary. It ended pretty bad, you know."

Kit didn't know the specifics of their parting, but she knew heartbreak when she saw it. "Yeah, but a lot of time has passed. You've both changed. You're different now," she offered. At that moment, she realized it was true. Milo's frenetic goofiness, like Jonathan's innate gloom, had diminished over time. Each of them transformed, more at home in their own skin.

"I probably love him," Milo blurted. He covered his mouth to unsay it, then his hand dropped away. "I do love him." He sucked in a breath. "Shit. I think I want to marry him."

Kit understood Milo's attraction. She, too, had once been smitten with the erudite professor. She'd girlishly perceived romantic overtures hidden within his every word, every gesture. Kit's naivety knew no limit. She'd never questioned Jonathan's sexual orientation—or anyone's, for that matter. Milo had been a platonic friend, more puppy than guy, and in all their time together, it never occurred to her he might be gay. Obviously gay people existed, but Kit hadn't known any personally—or so she thought. So, when she discovered the two of them nestled in post-carnal afterglow, the shock hit like a boot to the gut.

She lightly touched his hand. "Does he know how you feel?"

"Oh my God. Should I tell him?"

Kit smiled. They did make a handsome couple. She shook her head. "I don't know. I'm lousy at love."

Milo putt-putted into a parking place across the street from the Shell Station, cut the engine, and turned to meet her gaze. "Sorry, Kitty. I know you loved him, too."

She flushed. "That's ancient history. I can't believe I was such a goof."

"Yeah, but that's why I love you. You're brilliant," he said, poking her in the ribs, "but dumb as shit."

"Very humorous."

His face turned serious. "Speaking of love, when's the last time you saw Joe?"

"I haven't seen him," Kit said flatly. "Not since Humboldt." Silence hung in the air, sucking up all the oxygen. She rolled down her window. "The last I heard he moved to Santa Barbara for a teaching job at the university."

Milo mulled it over. "Santa Barbara's not very far. We could be there in five, six hours, tops."

The mere mention of Joe sparked a tingle. "You're right." She drew a sharp breath. "Probably a bad idea. I could never do it."

"Why not?"

"It's over," she said, aware that it was true, though her longing hadn't lessened. Joe had been the first guy she'd entrusted with her vulnerable heart. He'd been loyal and true, their sexual chemistry off the charts. But she'd thrown him away. By the time regret hit like a blow to the solar plexus, it was already too late. "Look, he's made it very clear; he doesn't want to see me."

Milo gave her a skeptical head tilt. "I bet you fifty bucks he does."

What if Milo were right? *What if* Joe still wanted her? She frowned at him. "You'd lose that bet."

"All I know is that you two were sickeningly in love—you were going to marry him, remember? That kind of love doesn't just die. I say go for it, Kit-Kat. Besides, I need a diversion. I think a road trip to Santa Barbara might be the ticket."

She frowned. "I'm glad you find my pathetic love life entertaining."

He gave her shoulder a squeeze. "I just don't want you to have any regrets, that's all. Look at me. I swallowed my pride and showed up at Jon's door. If I can do it, so can you."

"I'm not you," Kit said. Unbidden, a tear trickled down her cheek.

He draped an arm over her shoulder. "What have you got to lose?"

Kit had a good cry, giving into the sweet release. Leaning on Milo, she felt safe. The hard nut of her own stubborn will dissolved. "You're right," she breathed. "What have I got to lose?"

"Good. We'll go today."

Her heart quickened. "Maybe. No. It's complicated. There's the rental car. I have a job, an apartment."

"Steady, tiger," Milo cut her off. "One thing at a time, yeah? We'll deal with your car, then we can figure the rest out." He paused for a breath. "By the way, have you called your dad? He's probably crazy worried by now."

Kit squinted at him. "Jesus, when did you become so responsible?"

"Well, I am in my thirties, dear child."

"My God, we're so old."

"Yes, we are, my fellow Aquarian."

It dawned on her. "That's right. Our birthdays are coming up." Kit would turn twenty-eight on Valentine's Day. She did the math. Holy hell—that meant Milo would be thirty-three, and she guessed Jonathan was pushing forty. She glanced down the street to the bus stop, where the makeshift altar to John Lennon remained. It struck her now as a hauntingly beautiful testament to the fleeting nature of time, a life cut short. "God, how did we get here?"

Milo treated her to one of his brilliant grins. He shrugged. "I sure as hell don't know."

"I guess nobody knows."

"I know one thing. My ass is getting numb. We can't sit in this car forever."

On that note, Kit threw the door open and jumped out.

As they jaywalked across the busy street, Milo grabbed Kit's hand, a gesture so casual it made her eyes well up, his familiar ease an all-too-salient reminder of what she was missing. In New York she'd found a few female cohorts, a couple of temporary boyfriends, but not one true friend.

They stood on the pavement by the gas pumps and faced the garage. Milo pointed out a huge blue Ford. "Is that your rental?"

Kit chuckled. "Not even close."

Kit inhaled the sharpness of grease and metal. Her eyes traveled beneath the car to Ben, his body bent at an awkward angle, as if struggling to loosen a stripped bolt. "Hello?" she ventured.

Ben rolled out from under the car, rose to his feet, and straightened his coveralls. He gave Milo the once-over, as if sizing up the competition, then turned to Kit. "I found a bumper in a junkyard, but it's over in Oakland."

The man did not mince words. "That's great," Kit said.

Ben glanced at Milo again. "A friend of mine can pick it up, but he won't be able to bring it for a day or two."

Milo fidgeted like an overgrown kid. "I have a truck," he said.

Kit flushed. "Ben, this is Milo—an old friend of mine." Why she felt compelled to explain their relationship eluded her.

Milo extended his hand. "More like her big brother," he said.

"Cool," Ben said.

That Same Day
San Francisco

Jonathan waited with growing impatience for his hawkish agent, Arthur Zimmerman, head honcho of A to Z Literary, to swoop in. Aware of Art's legendary reputation for "fashionable" tardiness, he'd planned accordingly, showing up fifteen minutes past the appointed hour. But forty-five minutes hence, he deemed Art's lack of social graces egregious, even for him. The capper—he hadn't remembered to bring a book.

Had he gotten it wrong? It was possible, he supposed. When Nadia, the new girl, had phoned to set up the meeting, he'd been preoccupied, harried, at the stove cooking Dylan's cheesy eggs. Dylan bolted in, picked up the phone, then, looking mildly crestfallen, handed it to his dad. "Pop, it's for you," he'd said before retreating to his room.

Jonathan picked up. "Yes?"

Nadia had gotten right to the point. "Mr. Zimmerman will be in San Francisco next Monday. Are you available for a meeting?"

He'd stretched the cord to its limit, returned to the stove and switched off the burner. His doorbell began buzzing repeatedly, urgently. He'd been meaning to replace the offending buzz with a melodic ring but hadn't gotten around to it. With one hand covering the mouthpiece, he'd shouted to Dylan to wait for him before answering the door.

When Dylan didn't reply, he cut Nadia off. "Got it, one thirty, Café Georges," he'd told her before striding off. Flinging the door open, he'd discovered a vinyl siding advert rolled into the railing. He tossed it into the bin and experienced an off-kilter moment of doubt. He'd admitted then that he hadn't been paying attention to Nadia. He'd been distracted by her gum-smacking and nearly unintelligible Brooklyn accent, not to mention the doorbell.

His jaw tensed. Now what? Continue waiting or take off?

As Jonathan gazed into the dreggy bottoms of his second cup, a disembodied voice sawed through his musings like a chainsaw splitting a limb.

Zimmerman hovered above him, hand extended. "Wakefield, good to see you."

Jonathan rose to shake a cool, dry hand. "Art, good to see you, too." He paused. "I'd almost given up on you."

"I apologize, man. I grabbed a cab straight from SFO." He frowned. "Traffic was shit."

Jonathan took in Zimmerman's exterior: the ill-fitting suit, paisley tie, his hair arranged in an obvious comb-over. For a poorly groomed man of short stature, he managed to convey the confidence and authority of a much sharper-looking man.

Art glanced at his watch. "Shit," he said. "Better get started." Then he pulled up a chair, took a seat and signaled to the waitress.

Jonathan settled in, meeting Art's gaze. "How long are you in town?"

"Just today. Damage control," he said with a knowing smirk, as if the two of them shared some inside joke.

Had Zimmerman's notorious bicoastal escapades—the long-suffering wife in New York, the long-term paramour in San Francisco—finally unraveled? Jonathan wondered but didn't ask. While he didn't condone the man's conduct, he couldn't deny his own duplicity, his farce of a marriage to Kara.

The waitress arrived with a menu. "What can I get for you?" she asked, her boredom undisguised.

"Just coffee," Art told her, then had a change of heart. "How's the lemon pie, honey?"

She shrugged. "It's fine."

"Bring me a big slice, doll," he said before turning his full attention to Jonathan. "How's the novel coming?"

Jonathan flinched slightly. "It's going well."

"Do you think you'll meet the deadline?"

"I expect to," he said obliquely.

Zimmerman's brow furrowed. "I can't ask for another extension. I'm negotiating the advance as we speak. Wakefield, we're talking six figures easy. But you have to deliver."

The concept had come to him unbidden, a semi-autobiographical novel with a gay male protagonist. Initially the words had streamed out, like water flowing. But drawing closer to the unknowable plot, as if sinking in quicksand, he'd hit an impasse. "Understood."

Zimmerman's pie arrived and he tucked in. "Tart," he said with a sour face. He set his fork back on the table. "Bottom line, I need that draft yesterday." He slid the plate away. "It's fucking Random House, Jon, you're under a two-book contract. I've known Marty for years. He won't hesitate to drop you if you miss another deadline."

Jonathan felt a pang of longing for Zelda, his former agent—not a snake. The woman's advanced degrees in English and Russian literature had earned her reputation for her keen literary acumen. He doubted Zimmerman ever bothered to read. "Drop me? That's quite extreme, isn't it?"

Zimmerman fixed a look of real concern on his face. "If we don't deliver, he'll walk."

Jonathan narrowed his gaze, toying with the idea of dumping him here and now. Instead, he took a deep breath, let it out. Regardless of Zimmerman's crude reputation, he couldn't deny that his predatory instincts delivered. The last book had paid for his apartment and Dylan's future tuition. Jonathan held his tongue, cooling the self-righteous virtue. He couldn't afford to gamble with his livelihood. "You'll have the draft by the first."

"Excellent." Art rose to his feet, tossed a twenty on the table. "I'll ring Nadia, let her know to expect your manuscript."

Jonathan stood, following Art's lead. "Good to see you, Art."

Zimmerman extended his hand for a perfunctory bro shake. "I'll be in touch," he said. "Are you heading out?"

Jonathan regarded him. "You go ahead," he said. "I need to use the gents."

He settled back into his chair, and the sight of the uneaten lemon pie, slightly liquefied, made him queasy. Nevertheless, when the waitress drifted by with her pot, he accepted yet another refill. He checked his watch. Ten minutes, he decided, would provide an adequate buffer. The last thing he needed was a sidewalk run-in with Zimmerman—hailing a cab, soliciting a prostitute, kicking a puppy, or whatever he did when left to his own devices. Jonathan could think of nothing more agonizing than having to navigate a second cringe-worthy encounter with the man. He waited long enough to finish his refill before heading out the door. A wind kicked up, carrying the rousing scents of salt and decaying kelp. He glanced up at the sky to witness inky clouds gathering, swollen with rain. An ominous stillness hung in the air.

Jonathan hurried to the parking garage as fat little blobs of icy rainwater dotted the concrete, foreshadowing the torrent of rapid-fire hailstones that would pelt him and sting his cheeks. Eyes on the ground, grumbling as he advanced, he cut a sharp corner and crashed into a solid, fleshy mass.

"Christ, asshole. Watch where the fuck you're going. You could've knocked me down."

Jonathan stopped dead, coming face-to-face with a disheveled, fierce, wild-eyed woman. His insides clenched. "My God, I'm terribly sorry."

She smirked as if she'd heard it all before. "Yeah? Stuff your sorry and go fuck yourself." She turned on her heels and continued walking.

Jonathan stood dumbstruck, hail pelting his head. He eyeballed the woman as she scuttled down the sidewalk unsteadily. Then it hit him. "Hey!" he shouted.

The clouds parted to reveal a startlingly pale glimpse of sunlight, the faint chimera of a rainbow. She did an about-face, her stance *Dirty Harry* defiant. "Yeah?"

He approached gingerly. "I'm really sorry for bumping into you."

She remained stony.

"Look, I believe we're neighbors. I live across the street from you."

She cocked her head, squinting at him. "So?"

An inch of dark roots crowned her drenched, coppery hair. Jonathan was reminded of a pathetic calico cat. Her clothing was soaked, her white sneakers muddied. It pained him to look at her. "Can I offer you a ride? My car is in the garage, just a couple blocks from here."

She looked him up and down, her face pinched.

"Totally up to you," he said.

She studied him, appearing to weigh her options.

He could only imagine what she was thinking—to remain shivering and wet or take a ride with a creep.

After a long moment, she shrugged. "Fine."

Jonathan realized the outsized bag she slung over one shoulder partly explained her ungainly walk. He wondered what on earth she felt compelled to lug, and when she tossed it into the front seat, it made for cramped quarters. The Volvo had gone cold, and when he started it up, mutual discomfort and steamy breathing instantly fogged up the windows.

As he switched on the defroster, he stole a glance at her pale freckled arms. In his estimation, the woman weighed about as much as Dylan. "Aren't you going to buckle up?" he asked.

Without comment, she fastened it.

As he backed up, the windshield cleared, and he breathed a little easier. "So, what brings you to the Presidio?" It came out too cheery, a lame attempt to break the ice.

"Work."

Of course, he remembered stopping at her tollbooth, but still asked, "Where do you work?"

"The bridge."

Her snub at the tollbooth remained vivid in his mind. Apparently, it had never registered in hers. Jonathan rolled out of the parking structure. "You're kind of far from the bridge."

She released a noisy, weary exhale. "My car's in the shop. I took the bus to work, then I took another bus to my son's place, okay? Anything else you want to know? My fucking life story?"

He tightened his grip on the steering wheel, his shoulders hardening like stone. "Got it. No more small talk." Jonathan stewed in silence, muttering an internal monologue of woe. *No good deed goes unpunished. At the very least, she could feign civility. He did not have to put up with this shit.* "Look, I certainly didn't want to offend you."

Out of the corner of his eye, he perceived the slightest quiver of her left shoulder. She let out a choked sniffle. Was she weeping? He dared not wonder. He kept his gaze on the road, but it was impossible to ignore her muffled sounds of human suffering. Against his better judgment, he turned to her. "You okay?"

She dug into her enormous bag, pulled out a tissue. "Not really," she said. She laughed dryly, as if releasing some twisted agony. "I've had a pretty lousy day."

He nodded. "Sorry."

She blew her nose quietly into the tissue. "Thanks."

He noted a shift in her demeanor; not exactly warm, but no longer hostile. "By the way, I'm Jonathan," he offered.

"Beth," she said.

Silence lingered, but the air between them had cleared. At last, Jonathan turned into his driveway. "Here we are."

Beth collected her beast of a bag. "Thanks for the ride."

The transformation struck him. She'd visibly softened, her appearance markedly different from the nutjob he'd smacked into on the sidewalk. If he had to wager a guess, he'd place her in her mid-forties. Not young, not yet old. "You're very welcome," he said.

She released a breath through pursed lips. "Sorry for, well, being such a bitch. It's been a rough year, you know?"

"I do know," he said. "Anything I can do to help?"

She gave him an impish grin. "A new car would be nice."

When she smiled, she looked almost pleasant. "Well, at least I can offer you a ride now and then."

She opened the passenger door, stepped out. "I just might take you up on that," she said.

Jonathan waved to her as she crossed the street, but she didn't wave back. Perhaps she didn't see him. He climbed the staircase with heavy feet. The meeting with Zimmerman had drained him. Beth had also left him worn. With visions of cool sheets and cozy blankets, he slogged into the kitchen for a pre-nap snack. He did a double take when he spotted Katherine seated at the breakfast nook.

"Hey, you," she said.

She radiated happiness, grinning like a girl who'd won the lottery or stumbled into an unexpected windfall. He couldn't help but smile. "I take it you had a good time with Milo?"

"The best," she said.

"I'm glad."

She fiddled with her hair as if nervous, then gave him a tentative smile. "If it's still okay with you, I'd like to take you up on your offer."

Caught off guard, he choked up a little. "Of course, it's more than okay." He steadied himself, kept his emotions in check. "I'm delighted."

"Me, too," she said as she stood to embrace him. "I can't thank you enough."

Holding her, he breathed in her girlish herbal shampoo. The scent carried him back to Humboldt State, to young Katherine, his most promising student. He released her. "No need to thank me," he said.

She tucked a runaway strand of hair behind her ear. "I promise to be quiet as a mouse. And I want to pitch in—with money and cooking, and I can watch Dylan."

The weariness came again. "Not to worry. If you'll excuse me, I need to prepare for my class." He suppressed a yawn. "Talk later?"

"Sure. Can I make you a caffeinated beverage?"

"No, thanks. I've had about a gallon today."

With that, he gave up on napping and headed into his study. Thumbing through the pages of his lecture notes, it dawned on him. The solitary existence he'd taken for granted, both the isolation and privacy, had come to an end. Unbidden, his path had taken an unexpected jag. Beyond all reason, Milo had shown up like some beautiful dream. And for better or worse, Katherine Hilliard had become his roommate.

San Francisco
Later That Week

Milo devoured the last triangle of buttered toast, dabbed his lips with a napkin, and pushed his plate away. "Delicious, hon," he said. "Seriously, how do you do it?"

Jonathan's face brightened. "Anytime you want a cooking lesson, just say the word."

Kit took a sip, savoring the best brew she'd ever tasted. Until now, her experience with the bean had been limited to the powdery instant variety, Folgers in the red can if she felt like splurging. Jonathan's discerning palate, his taste, had made her a convert to the growing religion of California cuisine. "I'd take that lesson. Count me in," she said.

Milo pondered her. "Kit, as I recall, you're a great cook."

"I was. These days, I mostly heat cardboard meals in the microwave."

Jonathan looked as if he'd swallowed a mouthful of vinegar. "I'm disappointed in you, Katherine," he playfully scolded. "Microwaves are the spawn of the devil; they ought to be outlawed."

Jonathan and Milo smiled knowingly at each other, a gesture so intimate, so electric, Kit had to look away. All morning she'd picked up on a vibe, a subtle shift between the two of them. Milo insisted they were *taking it slow*, but if her romance barometer served, they'd surpassed *steamy* and were headed straight for *hot*.

"Jon is an anti-microwave zealot," Milo quipped.

"No, I'm a rational person who happens to prefer fresh fare that hasn't been electrocuted into lifeless pulp."

Milo gave Kit one of his sparkling grins. "Isn't this great?" he said. "It's like we're all back in Arcata sitting around your kitchen table having a lively debate."

Jonathan frowned. "You may be romanticizing those days."

But Kit knew what Milo meant. That funky Salvation Army kitchen table had been a focal point, attracting an ever-changing cast of characters, most of them friends of her kooky roommate, JJ. Her thoughts drifted, as they often did, to Joe. He, too, had been one of JJ's eclectic flock of friends. She would never forget the first time she laid eyes on him, the moment forever burned in her memory. She'd entered through the back door and was hanging up her coat when he'd materialized in the kitchen dressed in blue jeans and nothing else. Her eye had traveled from his brown eyes to his bare chest, settling at the waistband of his button-fly jeans, where her gaze lingered a beat too long. She'd flushed at the sight of his long black hair dripping wet from the shower.

Milo gave her a little shove. "Hey, Kit, where'd you go?"

"Sorry. I was thinking about the old kitchen."

"So, what do you think, is Jonathan right? Am I romanticizing those days?"

"Maybe," she said. She paused, considering it. "But I wouldn't trade it."

Milo bestowed her another winning smile. "Nor I, Kit-Kat."

"And now we're living the sequel," Jonathan said.

"Yes, but is it a drama or a comedy?" Kit asked.

Jonathan thought it over. "I'd call it a sitcom."

"*Three's Company* with an edge?" Milo suggested.

When the two of them made goo-goo eyes at each other, Kit rose to her feet. "I'll get the dishes."

"Leave them," Jonathan protested.

But she'd already started filling the dishpan with hot soapy water. "It's my turn," she said. "I have to earn my keep." She welcomed the homey chore, grounding her to the present.

Milo spoke to Jonathan. "Are you sure you won't come with us?"

Jonathan shook his head. "I'd like to, but Dylan's school concert is tonight. He's doing a violin solo."

Kit rinsed a plate, placed it in the drainer. "Really? I hate to miss that."

"Well, if the ensemble is anything like his last school band, you're not missing much."

"What's his solo?" Milo asked.

"A stirring rendition of 'Turkey in the Straw,'" Jonathan said proudly.

"I'm sure he'll be the best one," Kit said.

"I agree," Milo said. "Kit-Kat, are you ready to hit it?"

She dried her hands on a flour sack towel. "Almost. Just give me a second to pack up." With that, she shouldered open the door, trundled down the staircase, and rounded the corner of the main house to the little studio. Time was ticking. Kit focused intently on the task at hand, collecting her hairbrush, toothbrush, and a change of clothes. Shoving everything into the nylon backpack Jonathan had loaned her, she stopped short. Her chest tightened. What the fuck was she doing?

She'd only just arrived in San Francisco. Now she'd allowed herself to be swept away, blindly following Milo on one of his ill-conceived capers, like the time he convinced her to break into the dean's office. A chilling panic needled her skin. This was happening—this was real. She had no idea if they'd even be able to find Joe. And if they did, what if he didn't want to see her? *What if* he didn't love her? Then a whole flock of *what ifs* flew in, flitting and fluttering in her head. Her stomach turned. She should have skipped that last slice of bacon.

Kit took a deep breath, centering herself. She visited the bathroom and was washing up when she realized Milo had been right about one thing. She and Joe *had* been "one of those" rather annoyingly perfect couples. Joe had been the only one to ignite a fire in her. He'd made her tingle, made her laugh, made her think. Through the lens of hindsight, she understood now. This type of chemistry was rare—she'd been a fool to let him go.

As she recalled the morning of their fateful goodbye, her stomach bottomed out. She'd pledged her heart, given her word. Grief gnawed at the pit of her stomach, and for this agony, there was only one cur. She simply had to see Joe. She had to apologize, to try and salvage all she'd lost. Her desire was bodily, visceral, like a PMS craving for chocolate. Why bother to fight it?

The minibus sputtered noisily down Nineteenth Avenue. Milo's atypical silence created a disquieting void, a vacuum charged with Kit's nervous energy. At a loss, she nudged him. "What's going on in that curly head of yours?"

"Hmm?"

She shoved his bicep. "Hey, I asked you a question."

Milo nodded.

"Remind me why the hell we're doing this. Seriously, I'm freaking out about seeing Joe." She shoved him again. "Talk to me, okay?"

"Okay, Kit-Kat," he said absently.

Milo the legendary chatterbox remained mute, leaving Kit rattled and perplexed, stewing in her own volatile mental juices. Running down every worst-case-Joe scenario, she worked herself into a lather. For effect, she let out a moan. "Milo, I think this is a bad idea. I want to go back, okay?" She gave him a shove. "Do you even hear me?"

"Sorry," Milo said. "I hear you. It's just the traffic."

Kit regarded her friend, eyes fixed on the road, hands clenched in a death grip on the steering wheel. Maybe Milo had his own troubles and wasn't ready to air them just yet.

"You okay?"

"I'm fine, really. I just hate driving in the city."

It finally dawned on her. Milo was born in the boonies, on the Hoopa "rez," as he called it. He'd spent most of life in Humboldt, a county bisected by a single highway running north and south. She knew he lacked city driving experience and Kit could relate. The first few times she'd navigated San Francisco's manic road mashup, the learning curve had been so steep, her brain had pretty much exploded. For this reason, she decided to cut him a little slack.

Her eyelids fell, softening her vision and quieting her mind. Concentrating on the sounds and motion of the bus, the hazy blur of shapes and colors outside her window, she nearly drifted off to sleep. When Milo stopped abruptly, Kit jerked to attention, her eyes wide as they passed San Francisco State University. She squinted at the oddly dormant campus on the lookout for students, professors, any sign of life, when an odious feeling crept in. "Shit!"

Milo flinched. "Jesus, what is it?"

"I totally forgot—it's December. What if Joe's university is on break? What if he isn't even in town?"

He squeezed her kneecap. "Don't be a negative Nellie. We will find him."

"I find your optimism grating," she said.

"At least I know what month it is."

"Hilarious," Kit grumbled. But she had to admit, Milo wasn't wrong. She'd seen the decorations, the lights, the triangle-shaped trees. Yet somehow none of it had registered. This left her unmoored, as if she'd slipped into some parallel universe. But why? Had her father's mortality—her own mortality—induced a mind-numbing shock, a temporary amnesia? She realized she'd yet to process her father's brush with death. The experience had left her shaken and off center. This certainly would explain her inability to perceive the very existence of Christmas, her favorite holiday. In fact, it would explain a lot.

Kit kept quiet to avoid distracting Milo as he navigated a series of tricky lane changes. It occurred to her, in addition to Christmas, she'd forgotten about her rental. She wondered if Ben ever got that bumper from the junkyard. What if he didn't? Kit silently chewed on this troubling thought, wondering what else she might have overlooked. Spotting the off-ramp for Pacifica, guilt rolled around her low belly like a cold little pinball.

"Pacifica. That's where your dad lives, right?" Milo said brightly.

The pinball wobbled. "Yeah."

"Want me to cut over?"

She did, but she didn't. The new proximity to her father provided comfort but also a degree of apprehension. She'd broken the news to him as gently as possible, but her rationale for leaving New York came out sounding flimsy, even to her. He hadn't scolded her or questioned her judgment, but he couldn't hide his concern. Deep down, she knew he'd never approved of rash behavior. On principle, neither did she. But had her decision been rash, or was it inspired? "I'd rather stop on the way back, if that's okay."

Milo downshifted, keeping to 101. "Your wish is my command."

"Thanks," Kit said, vowing to visit soon and often. This year, unlike the last few, she'd definitely show up for Christmas.

As the traffic snarl gradually unwound, the fog lifted, revealing the first glimpse of the bay.

Milo let out a breath. He relaxed his grip on the wheel. "Isn't it gorgeous? You sure won't get this view in New York, will you?"

Kit took in the silvery still waters. "You're right. It's beautiful," she said. "I've always loved this part of the drive."

Milo rummaged through a box of cassettes, plucked out *Ziggy Stardust*, and shoved it into the player. "This track always reminds me of my first boyfriend."

"Okay, I'll bite. Tell me all about it."

Milo, returning to form, began filling the air with chatter. Kit relaxed a little, settling in for the duration. They continued their journey thusly for the next few hours as nondescript farm towns—Gonzales, Greenfield, King City— rolled by. Despite Milo's entertaining anecdotes, time slogged, and Kit felt her resolve flagging. When they stopped in San Luis Obispo for gas and a pee break, she bought two cans of Pepsi and a fistful of red licorice.

The caffeine and sugar kicked in, lifting her mood and her courage. But when they hit Pismo Beach, Santa Barbara looming less than eighty miles away, reality sunk in. Her ass had gone numb from sitting, her legs ached for a walk, but she would have volunteered to prolong the agony. She would have sat in Milo's cramped cab for eternity to escape facing Joe. Alas, too soon the exit for Santa Barbara emerged.

"We made it," Milo said as if she didn't have eyes.

Kit swallowed hard. "Now what?"

Milo pulled off the freeway, turning into the first shopping center they came to. He parked by the Safeway. "You mean to tell me you don't have a plan?"

Her mind blanked. "Not really." She glanced out at the horizon, pink and orange streaking the slate-gray sky. After a beat, she pointed to the phone booth in front of the market. "Square one, I guess."

Milo shrugged. "Worth a try."

She'd found Jonathan's number in the phone book. Could finding Joe also be that simple? What were the odds of hitting the jackpot twice? She took a deep breath, gathering her courage. "Come with me?"

He gave her a sunny grin. "You bet, Kitten."

On wobbly limbs Kit made her way to the booth. But weighing the hefty phone book in her hands, she lost her nerve. She handed the tome to Milo. "You do it?" she implored.

He regarded her skeptically. "Fine. It's Ito, right?"

"Yes, with an I," Kit said. "Joseph Ito." The name conjured Joe's unique features, his face an exquisite genetic meld. She never got the chance to meet his Japanese father, his Italian mother, or his kid sister. Joe's descriptions of his family had been so detailed that even now she felt as if she'd known them.

Milo flipped through pages and planted his index finger on the target. "Got it," he announced.

Kit blanched. "You're kidding."

He jotted down the number on a rumpled sales receipt and handed it to Kit. "Need a dime?"

Struck by a sudden bolt of decisiveness, Kit squared her shoulders. "No, I want to go to his house."

Milo wrapped her in a bear hug. "There she is. There's my girl," he said, patting her back like a bongo drum.

Milo ducked into Safeway for directions and Kit's determination hardened. In short order, they were back on the road and found Joe's street without a hitch.

"How are you doing?" Milo asked.

Kit's mission crystalized. Jumping into deep water beat sitting by the pool. "I'm good," she said. She scoured the terrain for Joe's place amid dozens of lookalike homes. The street narrowed, veering left. Eventually the houses thinned out, then disappeared altogether. Kit gazed at a stand of eucalyptus marking the border of the dead-end street. "Are you sure you have the right number?"

Milo braked, coming to a full stop. "I'm positive."

"Maybe it's a cosmic trick. Joe and his house exist in some parallel universe," Kit said.

"Very *Twilight Zone*, Kit-Kat," Milo said as he slowly drove to the outer edge of the street, circling back in the opposite direction. "What's the number?" he asked for the umpteenth time.

Kit glanced at the scrap of paper. "1-8-8-5," she said, her tone weary.

Milo brightened. "Look," he said, pointing beyond an overgrown hedge to a tiny white-stucco house.

Kit squinted at a house set back from the street and barely visible in the dusky light. The number on the mailbox confirmed it. Her body tingled. "This is it."

Milo set the parking brake. "Ready?"

Kit nodded. "Wait here, okay?"

"Are you sure?"

She glanced in the rearview mirror and attempted in vain to tidy her hair. "I'm sure."

Kit breathed deeply and gathered her courage. She headed down the long gravel driveway, cutting over to a cracked, weedy concrete path. With now-or-never tenacity, she climbed the stairs to the front porch. She pulled back the screen door and gave the wooden one several sharp knocks. She waited for a long moment, then rang the bell. Waited, rang again. Nothing. Her darkest fears and deepest insecurities came crashing in, her body flooding with shame. What a colossal mistake. Who did she think she was, showing up after nearly five years? Why on earth would he still want her? Her hand slipped from the screen door. As she turned to run away, the door slapped shut.

Kit scuttled down the pebbled driveway with steely single-minded determination. *Get to Milo, get the hell out of here.* But as she drew closer to the shelter of her best friend's arms, she caught sight of a man ambling down the sidewalk, a paper grocery bag nestled in the crook of his elbow. Kit weighed the visual evidence but refused to believe her own eyes. She drew a tight, shallow breath. She froze in her tracks and watched in horror, helpless to prevent Milo—the traitor—from jumping out of the car and waving his arms like a nutjob.

Milo yelled, "Joe!"

When Joe recognized the curly-headed kook, his face paled. Clutching his groceries to his chest, he turned to Kit, shock and incredulity registering on his face. "Kit?"

Feeling caught, Kit willed herself invisible. "Hi, Joe," she said, her voice catching.

His expression softened into a smile. He set his groceries down and made his way to her, giving her a quick, chaste hug. "What are you doing here?"

"I was in the neighborhood?"

Joe took a step back. "Do you want to come in?" He turned to Milo. "You, too, of course."

Kit glared pointedly at Milo. For once in his life, he took the hint.

Thinking on his feet, Milo spun some yarn about wanting to check out a surf shop. With that, he climbed into the van and took off, leaving Joe and Kit alone on the sidewalk, their shadows bathed in the pink glow of the setting Santa Barbara sun.

That Same Day
San Francisco

With Katherine and Milo's departure, a pleasant hush fell over the apartment. Jonathan, eager to get back to his novel, had welcomed the solitude. But as the hours disintegrated, the silence had grown stale and Jonathan ponderous. Zimmerman's unveiled threat—meet the deadline or else—replayed in his head like a broken record. Hell, he'd taken a decent stab at it. He'd picked apart paragraphs and killed entire scenes, then ultimately stalled.

"Give it a rest, Wakefield," he muttered to himself.

Resigned, he approached the stack of student papers he'd been avoiding. He plucked a paper from the stack and began to read. As he turned to page two, his eyes glazed. He would have welcomed one of Katherine's self-effacing, apologetic interruptions—any excuse to put down his grading pen. He envisioned the two of them head-to-head at the breakfast table plotting. Their mission: to track down Joe, Katherine's former fiancé. Katherine had waffled, poor girl, up to the eleventh hour.

"I don't know," she'd said. "I can't just show up. Maybe it's a bad idea. What do you think, Jonathan?"

What did he think? But who was he to question Cupid's arrow? "Well, it's certainly a risk," he replied. "A romantic leap," he continued, glancing

76

pointedly at Milo, leaper of all leapers—shower-upper on ex-lover's doorsteps, no doubt the mastermind behind the journey.

Katherine's face had scrunched with uncertainty. "Jonathan, you think I'm crazy, don't you?"

Jonathan smiled. "Not crazy. Perhaps a bit half baked," he'd said to lighten the mood.

Milo patted her on the shoulder. "Don't second-guess it. You're fully baked, Kit-Kat."

In the end, Jonathan held his tongue, swallowing his misgivings with his last sip of orange juice. Knowing he couldn't stop her, he'd done what he could—sent her off with a good, fortifying breakfast.

He turned his attention to a lengthy short story authored by Rain, his weakest student. Halfway through page one, he struggled to follow the meandering, unfocused narrative. Had she learned nothing last semester? Turning to page two, his vision blurred. He set the paper back on his desktop and mashed his fists into his eye sockets. He gripped his grading pen and clicked the ball point in and out, in and out. One goddamn paper, Wakefield, then a fresh start in the morning, he bargained. Jotting his notes in the margins of Rain's paper, his brain continued to cogitate, turning and twisting the unresolved plot of his novel like Dylan's little fingers worrying his Rubik's Cube. In the end, no matter how he tweaked it, nothing lined up.

The Next Morning
Somewhere north of Goleta, aka Hell

Kit squinted out the windshield into the too-bright glare. The claws of a cheap-wine hangover scratched into her skull, and the crappy coffee Milo had procured wasn't helping. She'd suffered a shitty, restless night, tossing and turning in the sandpaper sheets at Motel 6 while Milo snored like a puppy. Having endured a night of his intermittent snorts, she was in no mood for his jerky stop-start driving. She muttered curses under her breath. "Jesus, you drive like an old man."

Milo downshifted, maneuvering the gear knob with his right hand, his cup between his knees. He passed the cup to Kit. "Hold this, would you?"

"Okay," Kit said. She gulped the last of her own foul brew, then took a sip of Milo's. "Ugh. How much sugar did you put in here, five thousand packets?"

Milo let out a fatigued groan. He made a sharp turn off the highway, careened into the parking lot of a deserted beach, and hit the brakes—hard.

Kit lurched forward in her seat. "Jesus, what are you doing? Why are we stopping here?"

He cut the engine. "Look, I know you're hurting, Kit-Kat. But seriously, can you quit griping? You're not the only person with feelings, you know."

78

Kit fixed her gaze on the gray, churning sea. Spotting a lone surfer in a black wetsuit, she followed his progress as he paddled beyond the break. "Sorry," she said.

Milo fiddled with a button on his shirtsleeve. "Do you want to talk about it?" he ventured.

She didn't. Determined to cling to the last fragments of sweet denial, she shook her head. "No."

"Fine," Milo said.

Kit's lower lip trembled. Against her will, a tear leaked out. She brushed it away like a housefly. "Can we just go now?"

"As you wish, Your Highness." Milo started up the car and headed back to the highway.

Kit bullied her sweatshirt into a pillow. She rested her head and closed her eyes, but couldn't stop the movie playing in her head, couldn't rewind the regret. The unspeakable chronology would forever haunt her, leaving scars that couldn't be erased.

First mistake: stepping across the threshold into Joe's little bungalow, choosing to ignore the queasy tingling in her gut.

"Come in," Joe says, setting his groceries on the dining room table.

She takes in the fine oak table with its matching chairs, the understated artwork above the fireplace—two framed full-color scientific illustrations of wild huckleberry vines. All the décor tasteful and ordered, a grownup's house. "Nice place," she manages.

They stand facing each other, the table a solid barrier between them.

Joe looks at her as if he's dreaming, hoping he'll wake up soon. "How did you find me?"

"Phone book," she says, reduced to monosyllables.

Joe continues staring weirdly, shaking his head. "But what brings you back to California?"

"I came to see my dad." She pauses. "It's kind of a long story. You'll never guess who I'm staying with."

He furrows his brow. "Milo?"

"Actually, I'm staying in San Francisco, in Jonathan Wakefield's studio."

"Your old prof?"

She nods.

He stares ahead, shakes his head. "I still can't believe you're actually here."

She taps the table with her hand. "Well, I'm right here."

He meets her gaze and clever banter deserts her, all pretense gone. "I've missed you."

Joe walks around the table, his manner pained. He takes her hands in his. "I've missed you, too."

Is he grimacing? Has her presence made him physically ill? Her heart feels bruised.

Joe frowns wearily. As if resigned, he embraces her. Not an "old pals" hug, but a lingering, sexual enfolding. His kiss inevitable, his taste familiar and arousing. He sinks into a dining chair and pulls her onto his lap. Her fingertips explore his dark hair, shorter now, and the curve of her palm grazes his cheek—exquisite, cool to the touch. She tastes his skin, his very essence.

He kisses her hard. "My God, you're even more beautiful."

"You are," she breathes.

Joe takes her by the hand, leading her to the couch. She feels his weight on top of her, as one dreamy kiss dissolves into another. He fumbles with the buttons of her jacket. She strips it off, then lifts her arms for him. He peels away her t-shirt, unhooks her bra. She finds his zipper, the worn denim fabric taut and straining. Aching for him, she tugs at his belt buckle.

Joe grabs hold of her wrist a little too hard, nudging her hand away. He lets out an anguished animal moan as if ill. "We can't," he says, his voice quaky.

"What's wrong?"

He sits up straight, his face tight. He can't look at her.

A sudden jolt startles Kit from her misery. "What was that?"

"Sorry, I hit a chuckhole," Milo said. He righted the van.

"He's got a goddamn girlfriend," she wailed at the top of her lungs.

Milo glanced over at her. "Sorry, Kitty-Kat."

Kit closed her eyes and tried to shake it off, but the taste of Joe's kiss lingered; his words still stung. "She's a fucking scientific illustrator," she spat. "Her name is Amelia."

"Damn. She sounds like a real cow."

"She's probably beautiful. Blonde, no doubt," she grumbled.

"What you need, honey, is ice cream—stat."

"Can't. I have to deal with shit. I need to call that Ben guy about the bumper. I'm thinking about going back to New York to try to salvage what's left of my life."

"That's crazy talk. You just got here. Besides, what would I do without you?"

Kit frowned. Milo was right. She'd been staying with Jonathan for less than a week, but somehow it felt weirdly longer. "You don't need me, Milo. You have your art. You have Jonathan."

"That's debatable," he said, his frown hinting at unresolved issues between the professor and him.

Wrapped up in her own drama, oblivious to Milo's concerns or anyone else's for that matter, Kit plowed on. "I never should have gone. I'm such an idiot."

"You're no such thing," Milo said. "I think you did the right thing. Now you can move on. You won't have to wonder what might have been."

Kit laughed sardonically. "Have you forgotten? Ignorance is bliss."

San Francisco
December 20
A Few Days Later

By midafternoon, Jonathan had abandoned his office for the kitchen. While chopping fresh rosemary, the sharp woodsy scent filling his senses, his thoughts turned to Katherine. In his opinion, she'd been shaping up as the ideal houseguest, noiseless and tidy with a penchant for solitude. Recently she'd made herself scarce, no doubt moping over Joe. After returning from Santa Barbara, she hadn't offered any specifics and he dared not pry, but her untidy hair, baggy sweatpants and bloodshot eyes had clued him in. Obviously, things hadn't gone according to plan. He hoped her heart would soon mend.

As if on cue, Katherine quietly slipped in. She'd changed clothes and brushed her hair, both good signs.

"Hi there," he said.

She grinned. "Hi. I'm going to make a sandwich. Want one?"

He noticed Katherine's slight build, her ferocity, as she yanked the refrigerator open. It seemed she lived on peanut butter. She smeared it on bananas, apples, nearly everything she ate. Dylan, too, adored the stuff, but Jonathan had never understood the appeal. "No thanks."

Katherine slapped together a sandwich dripping with honey and employed a paper towel for a plate. She eyed his chopping board. "What are you making?"

"Marinara," he said. "Dinner's around six thirty," he reminded her before she scurried back down to the studio.

He turned to the stovetop, a benign contentment washing over him. It was nice having people to cook for. He crumbled the rosemary into his fragrant sauce, tasted it again and added a dash of pepper, a splash of burgundy. Satisfied, he placed the wooden spoon on its rest, leaving the sauce to simmer on a low flame. After a quick tidy up, armed and ready to face down his novel, it dawned on him he'd forgotten to pick up bread.

Jonathan's mental gears turned, and before long he arrived at a brilliant solution. Milo's studio happened to be next to a terrific Italian bakery. But before he had a chance to pick up the phone, the back door wobbled and jerked open. Glancing up, he expected to find Katherine, but instead Milo drifted in.

Milo grinned in all his glory, a sight to behold. Jonathan visually devoured every inch of him, from the worn leather boots, faded jeans, and black t-shirt to that unruly mop of hair.

Milo casually tossed his jacket to the table. "Hi, handsome."

"I was just about to call you," Jonathan said. "To what do I owe the pleasure of this unexpected visit?"

Milo held his gaze. "I missed you."

Jonathan's heart thrummed in his ears. Countless times they'd been alone, even kissed in this very kitchen, but never had his knees turned to jelly. "I've missed you, too." He wrapped his arms around him, breathing in his uniquely Milo scent, earthy and citrus, with notes of Tide detergent. "But you're early, hon," he breathed. "Dinner's not till six thirty."

Milo moved in close, their lips brushing. "Or maybe I'm right on time."

Jonathan pressed a finger to his lips. "No more talk."

Together they stumbled down the hallway, gracelessly groping, fumbling with zippers and buttons. Jonathan managed to kick the door shut, then yank off his trousers before falling into bed.

Milo climbed on top and kissed him. "You taste goddamn delicious," he said.

Jonathan feasted on Milo's lips, his neck. "You do."

Face to face, flesh on flesh, Milo's curls falling on his face, Jonathan nearly came. He was so turned on, he dispensed with the kissing, urging Milo to go down on him with a shove of his hand. It hadn't been his most suave move, but in his defense, he thought, it had been a while.

After taking care of Milo, spent from sheer exertion, his pulse still racing, Jonathan rolled over on his side, their naked limbs lazily intertwined.

Milo gave him a tender kiss. "I should pop in more often."

Up close, Milo's features blurred. Jonathan couldn't discern where he left off and Milo began, their breath and hearts one. "Being with you feels like coming home."

Milo caressed his face. "You're sweet."

Without seeing Milo's face, Jonathan sensed he was smiling. He breathed into Milo's ear. "Yes, and next time I will be even sweeter."

"What's your hurry, tiger?" Milo teased.

"I suppose you have a point. The best things in life take time," Jonathan conceded.

Milo nibbled his lower lip a little too hard. "I'm willing to go slow."

Jonathan allowed the current to take him. Time liquefied. Hair and skin and heat. Kissing, fucking, drowning. Coming up for air, he moaned, then rested his head on the pillow. He stared blearily at the white plaster ceiling, looked to the window and the dusky light outside. An afternoon gone; hours dissolved. He couldn't explain where the time had gone, which left him vaguely unsettled, yet he'd never felt more at peace. He turned his head to get an eyeful of his beautiful man. Gazing languidly at the fine hairs on Milo's upper arm, his smooth skin, the strapping cut of his bicep, Jonathan relaxed into the afterglow.

Milo nudged him. "Jon, do you smell something burning?"

Jonathan jolted up. "Shit, my sauce!"

"I'm sure it's fine," Milo said.

Jonathan shook his head. "Unlikely," he said. He arose and reached for his trousers.

Milo grabbed him by the arm, pulling him to the bed. His face turned sober. "Wait a second, Jon."

"What? What is it?"

Milo looked directly into his eyes. He took his hand. "I want us to commit. I think we should live together."

The words floated for a beat, slowly sinking in, then landed like a peach pit in the bottom of Jonathan's belly. "Live together? A little fast, don't you think?" he managed.

Milo's face went taut. He dropped Jonathan's hand. "Why do you always do this?"

Jonathan understood perfectly what he meant, but asked, "Do what?"

Milo wore a pained expression as if gathering the patience needed to explain a difficult algebraic concept to a dull five-year old. "We get close. Then you push me away."

Jonathan's vision tunneled. "Sorry," he mumbled. "I can't do this now. I need to check the stove."

Like the coward he was, he fled. Upon entering the sanctuary of his kitchen, he caught a whiff of an off-putting metallic scent, confirming that his sauce had indeed scalded. Ruined, like so many things he'd touched.

He got to work doctoring the sauce, adding red wine, tomato paste, then stirring. More wine, more stirring. Perhaps the sauce was salvageable. His relationship, on the other hand, had no foreseeable cure. Jonathan couldn't keep kidding himself. Milo's patience wasn't limitless. He would grow weary and eventually split—this time for good.

Was he even capable of forming a lasting commitment? Could he trust himself to hold on to the man he cherished? The idea left him petrified, knowing he must find a way to mend the rift he'd made.

Jonathan turned the pages of the new Joan Didion book without reading. The evening had been a disaster. Milo left before dinner and Katherine never did show up. He admitted that Milo had been right. Jonathan had always ruined love. He'd never learned how to trust or be trusted.

It hadn't been for lack of trying. He'd wanted more than anything to make his marriage work, compartmentalizing his affairs, juggling lies. He might have pulled it off, too. But he'd overestimated Kara's undying devotion, underestimated her sleuthing ability. When Kara found out about Raj, she'd quit pretending and stripped away all his covers, leaving him exposed.

He swallowed painfully. It wasn't a goddamn choice. Growing up in a midwestern conservative culture, he would have given a limb to make the urges stop, to cure the defect. His old man knew the truth, shipped him off to boarding school to toughen him up.

He wept, remembering his boyhood's end.

At fourteen, far from home, he experienced his first furtive sexual encounters, falling in love with Mason. Mason, who later called him a fucking faggot, and for good measure punched Jonathan's face bloody. For the remainder of his high school career, he took refuge in the library, earning a scholarship to Iowa. In undergrad, he hid behind his intellect. He'd pored over the American Psychological Association's *D.S.M.* with scholarly distance. The irrefutable facts stared him square in the face. Homosexuality was classified as a mental affliction, like schizophrenia. A felony, punishable by imprisonment, a perversion.

So, what did that make him?

Floundering, in desperate need of a cure, Jonathan returned to Minnesota. Willingly, prayerfully, he joined a Christian conversion therapy program. Hours of torture? Sure. Subject his genitals to electric shock? Bring it on. Anything to flush the demon out and make good.

And it worked. At thirty, he'd married Kara, gotten her pregnant. Case closed.

Five years in, he fled to Humboldt, ostensibly for a visiting author summer gig. A month later, to Kara's chagrin, he accepted a full-time position. Enter Katherine, his promising earnest student. Then her sidekick, Milo, free-spirit gay man-boy, out of the closet and into the light. Milo had seen through the straight act, the wedding band. A wisecracker, a mop-top clown, he stared directly into Jonathan's soul and didn't flinch. Milo had been younger, freer, more evolved, unafraid. Jonathan, nowhere near ready, drove him away.

Jonathan massaged his temples. Things were better now, weren't they? He'd changed, hadn't he? He'd come so far since those tortured days, right?

He rose from his chair, his back weary from sitting, his brain overwrought. With a yawn, he brewed a cup of chamomile tea and changed into his pajamas and robe. He thought about getting back to his writing, but instead reached for one of the books on his end table. Jonathan settled in for an all-too-quiet evening of books and tea, but his mind drifted to Milo again. He should be here with him, stretched out on the couch, looking gorgeous, stocking feet dangling over the arm. They belonged to each other. As he plotted his strategy to win him back, his heart lightened.

Night descended and he switched off the lights and crawled into bed. Lying in the dark, listening to his own steady breathing, he heard what sounded like a faint knocking on his front door. He checked the clock. Late, after midnight. The knock grew louder, persistent. His gut told him nothing good awaited him on the other side of the door. Best to ignore it.

The doorbell rang. It rang again.

"Shit," he grumbled, snatching up his robe.

Jonathan approached the door quietly and peered through the peephole. After a beat he recognized his neighbor on his doorstep. What was she doing at his house? He opened the door. "Beth, hello. What brings you here?"

Her demeanor was harried. Bathed in yellow porchlight, her face appeared wan. "You said if I ever needed a ride."

True, he'd made the offer, but hadn't bargained for a midnight rousting. "It's awfully late."

She began wringing her hands. "Look, I wouldn't ask if it wasn't an emergency." Her expression darkened. "It's my son."

"What's wrong?"

"The hospital called. I need to go—now, for fuck's sake. Will you take me or not?"

Perhaps he should have stayed in bed, left the door closed. But he'd opened it, and it could not be unopened. "Come in. Give me a minute to change."

Same Day
Same City

Kit flopped down on her bed, cursing her stupidity. How had she ended up in this bottomless well of angst? It all started, she reckoned, when she decided to leave Joe.

After finishing grad school at the tender age of twenty-four, a lifetime ago, Kit had *arrived*. To her utter amazement, she'd fulfilled every aspiration on her checklist, surpassing every one of her dreams:

1. Short story published in the *Paris Review*—check.
2. Debut story collection hot off the presses—check.
3. Diploma from a reputable college—check.

With a yawn, she recognized she'd been starry-eyed back then. When Zelda, her mentor and champion, offered her an entry-level position at Greene Literary Agency, she'd called it a stepping-stone, her entrée to the New York publishing scene, a chance to hobnob with the exclusive heavy hitters. In short, a coup. The offer, both flattering and thrilling, had been too good to pass up. Nevertheless, Kit's decision hadn't been easy—it hadn't been a straight line.

After NYU, Kit had planned to return to California to marry the sweetest, smartest, most loyal guy on the face of the earth. It was airtight. Then Zelda tossed a monkey wrench in the works, the offer tearing Kit apart. Whatever she chose had felt like it would have been a betrayal, either to Joe or to herself. In the end, she couldn't bear the thought of looking back in twenty years wondering what might have been. She'd made her choice. Unclasping the gold chain, she'd removed Joe's promise ring. Dropping it in the mailbox felt like severing a limb.

The following Monday Kit had embarked upon her new career—her new life, the bright summer morning still vivid in her mind. Ascending the marble staircase, her palm grazed the polished hardwood banister. She entered the cheery little office with its scholarly coffee-scented vibe certain she'd made the right choice.

The early days had been halcyon, dreamy, and intense. Dimly lit bars, brilliant, bearded guys smoking cloves. The world took on a glamourous patina, as if she'd landed in a late-night movie, an endless montage of black-and-white newspaper headlines: "California Girl Takes NY Publishing Scene by Storm," or "That Girl's Got Spunk!" Hell, she was Katherine Hepburn. Or in other incarnations, Mary Tyler Moore, a plucky gal starring in her own life. And like Mary, she approached her work with conscientiousness and aplomb. In her role as literary agent, Kit identified with the aspiring writers; she'd respected their courage and vulnerability. She combed every submission, even those with little promise, in search of hidden gems, crafted every rejection letter with carefully chosen words of encouragement, gentle critique.

She'd wanted to impress Zelda, but discovering the next bestseller proved more onerous than she'd imagined. Like all ambitious women in a male-dominated profession, Kit worked harder to shine than her male colleagues. To forget Joe, she immersed herself in her work, leaving no space for regret.

Once her male counterparts got the message she wasn't in the market for a man, they treated her like one of the boys. She liked that they didn't censor their crude jokes, liked the way they bounced around ideas, pumping each other's creative juices. The guys invariably claimed to be novelists or poets working at Greene on the side. They ate, drank, and breathed writing, like Kit, though they lacked her discipline. When the gang gathered for a night of drinking and carousing, Kit nursed a single gin and tonic, then slipped back to the office to craft her novel in solitude. Working into the wee hours, sometimes she ended up sleeping at the office and would wake up raring to go, exhilarated and more passionate than the night before. Kit had grown accustomed to ongoing blessings, so when Zelda summoned the troops to the conference room, she'd expected more good news, perhaps the acquisition of a sought-after, high-profile client.

In her naivete, she completely missed the obvious warning signs. The conference room had been quiet, the table oddly void of donuts. When Zelda entered, the very air in the room thickened. A vivacious woman of imposing height, Zelda typically wore her hair in a loose chignon held mysteriously in place by a pair of chopsticks. But that day, her hair hadn't been styled. She cleared her throat. "We had a hell of a good run," she'd said with a complete lack of sentiment.

Kit experienced a weird sinking feeling. She avoided eye contact with Zelda and the others, unable to process the unfiltered truth. Her beloved Greene Agency was folding. In an eye blink it was over. Rose-colored glasses shattered. Little did Kit know, an unseen chisel had already begun chipping away at the literary bedrock of her beloved New York, and publishing as the world knew it would never be the same.

After shuttering the agency, Zelda vanished, rumored to be recuperating in the Bahamas. Powell-Standish, the agency that had acquired Greene, offered to retain Kit as a "junior" agent. Out of options, she agreed to move uptown to the new corporate offices, all glass and sharp edges. She'd worked hard, waiting for recognition, waiting for her ship to come in, waiting . . .

Kit faced the mirror as she dragged a comb through her tangles. Now, confronting the hard facts, she realized the time had come. From this day forward, she would captain her own damn ship. She absolutely would.

But first, she needed to hear the sound of her dad's voice.

As if he'd been sitting by the phone waiting for her call, he answered on the first ring. "Hello?"

"Dad?"

"Hey, how's it going, honey?"

Kit heard the smile in his voice. She liked it when he called her honey, a reminder of innocent days, when she was a girl and he, her protector. "I'm good. More importantly, Dad, how are you?"

"Great, so much better." He paused. "I'd say I'm up to eighty-five percent."

He always quantified his health in percentages. "Eighty-five? That's a B+. Pretty good. And are you behaving yourself?"

"You know Cindy," he said, with a chuckle. "She's keeping me in line. Don't worry. I'm not eating anything remotely tasty."

"I take it you're still exercising?"

"Yep. But I do miss my walking partner."

"I'll come and see you soon," Kit said, though she wondered how she'd make the trip without a car. A moment of silence hung in the air while she considered the daunting prospect of starting her life from scratch.

As if he could read her thoughts, he asked, "How are you adjusting to San Francisco?"

Kit understood that her dad questioned her sudden decision to quit a good-paying job, upending her entire life, but he'd never criticized, never judged. "It's terrific," she fibbed.

Their conversation settled into a familiar rhythm, a father-daughter dance, of sorts. Sidestepping sticky subjects—beat—reassuring each other—beat—dodging pain.

Then her dad's tone turned solemn. "You know, Kath, you can always come home."

Kit brushed a tear from her eye. "Yeah, I know." And in that moment, she was grateful to let her dad steer the ship, albeit ephemeral, and for that, she loved him with all her heart.

San Francisco
December 23
Christmas in the Air

As Jonathan loaded the breakfast dishes into the dishwasher, Dylan barged into the kitchen.

"Dad, when is he getting here?"

"Any minute now, I'd guess."

Dylan wore a pouty look. "But when?" he asked for the umpteenth time.

Jonathan had to give the kid credit for persistence. He'd been monitoring the front window all morning on the lookout for Milo's truck.

Katherine placed a hand on Dylan's shoulder. "Want to go check again?"

"Okay," Dylan said, following her into the living room.

As Katherine pulled back the curtain, Jonathan joined them at the window.

"Hey, I think I see him!" Dylan cried.

"Told you," Jonathan said.

They all gawked at Milo's van as it backed into the narrow driveway and farted to a stop. Jonathan ruffled Dylan's hair. "Ready for an adventure, kid?"

Dylan squirmed away from his father's touch. "I've been ready for a century."

"A century?" Katherine said. "We'd better get a move on then."

"Don't forget this," Jonathan said, handing Dylan his coat.

The three of them clamored down the staircase. Milo's door swung open, and he jumped out. "Hey, all," he said. "Looks like you're ready to go."

Katherine buttoned her coat. "Someone's been ready for hours," she said, giving Dylan a pointed look.

Jonathan squeezed in first, the gear stick pressed against his knee. Katherine followed, taking the passenger seat.

"Where do I sit?" Dylan asked as he wriggled in.

Katherine pulled him into her lap. "I think you're stuck with me."

"All set?" Milo asked.

In unison, they responded yes, and off they went. Weaving through light traffic into the Presidio, Jonathan found Dylan's excitement contagious. Despite the cramped quarters, he felt liberated.

The boy squirmed in Katherine's lap. "I'm squished."

Jonathan chuckled. "We all are, buddy."

Dylan exaggerated a shiver. "It's also f-f-freezing. Can you turn on the heat?"

"No can do," Milo said. "Heater's busted."

Katherine wrapped her arms around him. "Is that better, my prince?"

"Better," Dylan said.

She gave him a little poke in the ribs, making him giggle.

Dylan's little boy laughter, like a feather, tickled Jonathan's ear. Today's record cold triggered faded memories of Minnesota winters, bright mornings bundled in heavy coats and mittens. Dylan, flushing with cold, shrieking with delight, sledding down the snowy little hill—again and again.

"Nice day," Katherine said.

Jonathan looked up at the sky, translucent clouds haloing the burnt-orange arches of the Golden Gate. He turned his gaze north to the craggy headlands lush from recent rains, the sparkling bay below. The breadth of California's natural beauty still startled him. He nodded. "Gorgeous day," he amended.

"You're right, it is gorgeous," Katherine said.

Jonathan noticed she'd been more upbeat lately, since her ill-fated encounter with her ex-boyfriend, Joe. He figured Milo may have something to do with her improved demeanor. Regardless, he was glad she'd decided to stay in California, at least through the holidays. Dylan had grown quite fond of her and would miss her if she were gone.

"Up here, Jon?" Milo asked.

"Yes, take the next exit," he said, pointing it out.

Milo cut over, taking Jonathan's halting directions through a maze of twisting, leafy Mill Valley streets.

"There it is!" Dylan cried, pointing out the hand-painted sign: *Zander's Farm.*

Milo made a left onto a tight gravel road, soon arriving at the farm. A convincing Santa held court in front of a quaint whitewashed barn decorated with twinkle lights. Cheery holiday trees of all sizes, both flocked and naked, filled in the scene. Dylan, unable to wait another second, threw open the door and tumbled out. Katherine followed suit, flung the door shut, and chased after him.

Momentarily alone in the cab with Milo, Jonathan turned to him. "Thanks for driving."

Milo nodded but didn't meet his eyes. "Wouldn't miss it."

They'd hardly had a moment alone since their last disquieting encounter. Every word, every gesture, had been fraught with subtext. Milo, never one to suppress his feelings, had shut down. He'd taken a chance, laying bare his vulnerable heart. *I want us to live together, Jon.* In return, Jonathan had wanted to hold him and tell him how much he loved him, but cowardice choked his voice.

Then Milo had split, leaving Jonathan to stir his marinara and stew in his own stale juices. *Two men cohabitating—what would his readers think? Obviously, they'd think he was a fucking fag.* Fear of exposure lay festering at the bottom, buried beneath a pile of lesser fears that had fossilized. He was afraid of moving in together. But the thought of moving forward alone, without Milo, left him feeling wretched and small.

The realization had been gradual, like ice melting on a cold winter's day. Then, all at once, it avalanched. Who fucking cared what people thought? Milo sparked him and made him think. Milo was devoted and loving—he was family. Jonathan would be of the lowest order to let such a man go.

Jonathan began, "Look, I've been thinking about what you said."

"You have?"

"Yeah," Jonathan said. "I think we should explore the idea."

Milo met his eyes. "Really?"

"Definitely."

"I know it's not easy," Milo said. "That big brainy head of yours gets cluttered like your desktop."

Jonathan chuckled. "It's like my desktop, only swampier."

Milo shook his head. "Now that's a graphic I won't soon forget."

Jonathan brushed a stray curl from Milo's brow. "Give me another chance?"

"I'm all yours," Milo said. He paused for a long moment. "Listen, we can take it slow, whatever you need."

Jonathan had no intention of taking it slow but didn't let on. With a start he remembered he would need to slip out to pick up the engraved silver key ring. Tomorrow was Christmas Eve. What time did the jeweler close? He squeezed Milo's hand. "Thanks for understanding."

Milo gave him a playful clap on the knee. "Let's get us a tree."

The chilly pine-scented air, not to mention the promise of love, heightened Jonathan's senses. He approached Dylan and Katherine, hotly debating the merits of a whopping noble fir.

Katherine squinted at the tree, shaking her head. "It is beautiful, but I don't think it will fit through the front door."

Dylan turned to his father. "What do you think, Pop?"

Taking in the child's cheeks, flushed from the cold, his searching, doleful gaze, he knew he was toast.

The Next Day
Christmas Eve

With Dylan safely tucked in bed, Jonathan prepared for Milo's arrival. He set out a plate of gingerbread, stoked the fire, placed a few wrapped boxes beneath the tree, and switched on the lights. Despite Dylan's preference for gaudy tinsel, he had to concede the decorations worked. Swathed in hundreds of twinkling lights and framed by the street-facing window, it truly was sublime.

With a chuckle, he recalled wrestling the massive fir into Milo's truck bed, then dragging it up the staircase into the apartment. The beast had taken over the living room, pine needles scattered everywhere. Jonathan figured he'd be cleaning them up well into July. It had taken hours to decorate—Dylan had been so worn out he'd gone to bed without prompting.

When it came to all things Christmas, his son favored the adage *bigger is always better*. While Jonathan did not share Dylan's viewpoint, he'd happily yielded, knowing all too well the fleeting nature of childhood. He would have given the kid the moon and stars, without hesitation, if only he could. For now, Dylan would have to settle for the Legos and telescope under the tree.

Jonathan put on some Christmas music to set the mood. He ambled into the kitchen, and as he stirred the cocoa warming on the stove, his thoughts meandered. It had been an idyllic, lazy day, he mused. Morning had arrived with gusty winds and drizzle. Jonathan had been at the window, watching the gathering storm, when Katherine entered the room bundled in her New York coat.

Katherine had placed a few little gifts beneath the tree, and with a hasty hug and little fanfare made her departure. She'd managed to procure yet another rental car—fingers crossed—to use while spending the Christmas holiday with her dad. A couple days ago, after the tree farm caper, Milo had split for Humboldt and wasn't due back until tonight. Kent and Kara had traveled home to Minneapolis, attending to Kent's ailing father, which meant that for the moment, Jonathan had Dylan all to himself.

With the storm brewing outside, they celebrated Christmas Eve snug and warm. He and Dylan had watched old movies, fiddled with the tree decorations, iced gingerbread men, and wrapped last-minute gifts. Around six o'clock, Jonathan had called in Chinese delivery, indulging Dylan with a double order of pot stickers and adding broccoli chicken for good measure. After dinner, a little TV, and Jonathan's traditional bedside reading of *A Visit from Saint Nicholas*, the boy was sound asleep by eight. Even though Dylan had long since eclipsed the magical thinking phase, father and son adhered to a tacit pact: if the existence of Saint Nick remained unquestioned, he would come.

Jonathan readied two Santa mugs, one for him and one for Milo. He checked the time and tapped his shirt pocket, confirming the presence of the little red box with its pretty bow. In keeping with his wary nature, Jonathan had overthought the gift. Glued to his desk, pen in hand, he'd rejected a number of ideas. In the end, he'd chosen a simple sentiment, one he believed fitting, commissioning the jeweler to engrave a single word: *Home*. He pictured the silver key fob with its attached shiny house key and imagined Milo's reaction as he opened the box. At first his face would register confusion, then he'd unleash that radiant smile.

The doorbell rang and Jonathan sprang from his seat, his heart hammering. He glanced at his watch again. Milo was early. He took a deep breath to calm his jitters, switched on the porchlight and flung the door open, finding not the love of his life, but Beth, his neighbor. His heart sank. Should have known better. Milo never rang the bell, preferring to barge in through the back door unannounced.

"Beth?" he said, unable to disguise his disappointment.

She handed him a paper plate wrapped in foil. "Merry Christmas," she said. "I saw your lights were on, hope it's not too late."

He took a long look at her. Bundled in her red coat, her cheeks flushed from the cold, she appeared younger and more vibrant, as if ten years had melted away.

She gave him a bright smile. "It's shortbread. An old family recipe."

"That's so kind of you. Thank you."

"No, thank you. I really appreciate you giving me that ride."

"It was no trouble." He glanced at the paper plate, heavy in his hand. Her neighborly gesture touched him. "Won't you come in?"

"Thanks, but I can't. Jamie's home."

Jonathan recalled his awkward encounter with Jamie, Beth's son. Less than a week ago, he'd driven Beth, frantic and consumed with dread, to the hospital. He'd accompanied her to her son's bedside and was shocked by the young man's gaunt, wasted appearance. Jonathan had suspected long-term drug abuse, perhaps an overdose, but didn't mention it to Beth. She'd had enough to contend with.

He met her eyes. "How's he doing?"

Beth gave him a weak smile. "Better. They pumped him full of antibiotics." She glanced across the street to her apartment. "I'd better run."

Jonathan nodded.

"Merry Christmas, Jonathan," she said, her breath vapory in the naked yellow light.

He gently squeezed her shoulder. "Merry Christmas, Beth."

ACT TWO

San Francisco

January 20, 1981

Dawn broke. Kit bundled up and made her way to the main house for a dose of caffeine. She brewed a pot and headed back down to the studio, balancing hot buttered toast and her sloshing mug. After a few missteps, the new year was shaping up quite well, she thought as she hunkered down at her little desk. Doggedly determined to purge the mental rust and get the juices flowing again, she'd been writing every day. Thus far the work had been unfocused and without clear direction, but she persisted, trying not to judge. Jonathan urged her to get back on the horse and set her sights on mainstream magazines in the market for essays or short fiction. She trusted his advice implicitly and acknowledged the value of his connections.

Kit started with a free-form writing exercise she'd learned in college that involved generating ten random nouns to use as a springboard. Her writing meandered from musings about living in the eighties to childhood and death, but around eleven o'clock, her attention flagged. Fingertips poised atop the keyboard of her new IBM word processor, she fixed her eyeballs on the page, but the screech and rumble of the garbage collector's truck shattered her concentration. Kit rose from her chair and took a long stretch. Could it be her author ship had sailed? Nevertheless, glancing out the window into Jonathan's little yard, she couldn't imagine a more ideal place—nowhere on earth she'd rather be. Her life was finally back on track. New year, new Kit.

She'd never given much thought to the spiritual realm. But recently she wondered if God's hand had played a part in nudging her back to California. Or had she simply stumbled into her new dream life, her cup overflowing with good fortune? Regardless of how she got here, she vowed to make the most of this gift.

Admittedly, the road west had not been without bumps. She'd reclaimed her life, but during the transition suffered growing pains and some of the shittiest days of her life. That's what she told herself as she wove her narrative, editing and memorizing it until it felt like truth. With a faraway look, she mentally replayed her story, piecing together all the little moments, the fragments of time.

It started abruptly with her dad's brush with death. That singular event changed everything. For the first time in her life, she'd realized her own mortality. It made her reevaluate the weighty consequences of life choices. The very real possibility of losing her father left her devastated. She'd been vulnerable and confused. In her fragile state, Joe's rejection was devastating and physically painful, like a kick to the gut.

Kit forgave herself for succumbing to grief and self-pity. But after a couple days of wallowing, she grew tired of her own circular thinking, her own wretched company. One morning, she noticed the pain had lessened. She simply made up her mind to quit moping and get the fuck on with life.

A holiday visit with her parents had also proved pivotal. On Christmas morning, strolling the deserted Pacifica shoreline arm in arm with her dad, it hit her. California was her home. She belonged here. In that very moment, the leaden dread she'd been carrying like a load of concrete released from her body. She felt energized, determined to tie every loose end—her apartment, her job—and as she boarded the redeye and buckled her seatbelt with a solid click, her grit strengthened.

On the second of January, Kit landed in New York. She saw gloom everywhere: gray skies clinging to gray littered sidewalks, a skinny gray cat slithering into the alley. She'd picked up her pace, barging into her building, the lobby overheated and smelling of stale tobacco. Kit had opened her overstuffed mailbox and tucked her *New Yorker* and phone bill into her shoulder bag. She gathered her courage, tramping upstairs for the last time.

Kit took in a ragged breath, slipped the key into the lock, and prepared for the worst. The air inside had grown chilly and stagnant as a fusty museum. Otherwise, it appeared exactly as she'd left it. The box of saltines discarded on the kitchen counter. Her cramped bedroom with its unmade bed. Her bathtub ringed with bubble scum. A life frozen in time.

She'd thrown open the bathroom window, cranked up the heat, rolled up her sleeves, and gotten to work. Snapped on rubber gloves, scoured the tile, toilet, sink, and tub. Next, she hit the kitchen, wiping down the countertops and cleaning out the fridge. She'd vacuumed the ugly carpet, dusted the worn furniture, packed up her clothing and meager belongings. At the appointed time, the superintendent rang her bell, and for her efforts, refunded her entire deposit—two hundred fifty bucks. Kit paused at the threshold to say goodbye to the apartment, her home for nearly five years, and closed the door like a book.

Steamer trunk in tow, she'd splurged on another taxi to Powell-Standish, her dad's words of advice an endless loop in her head. *Never burn a bridge.* As predicted, Dad had been right. In addition to her final paycheck, to her astonishment the grouchy shrew in personnel handed over $243.67, calling it severance. Kit quickly folded it into her wallet before they could realize their mistake. She couldn't help but wonder if Jonathan's connection with Robert Powell had facilitated this windfall.

Kit devoured the last crumbs of her toast. She'd bought the good bakery bread Jonathan liked, and although it was a little thing, it made her feel proud. Taking stock of her finances, Kit smiled. With the addition of her dad's Christmas gift, a whopping two thousand dollars, her checking account had never been this flush. She figured that if she minded her pennies, she'd have a year to make a go of writing. It went against her principles to freeload, so she made a point of chipping in for household expenses. She'd insisted on paying rent, and Jonathan grudgingly agreed to a hundred dollars a month—a fraction of her New York rental. The man's generosity knew no bounds. Because of him, Kit had found her momentum.

The icing on the cake: Milo. He'd recently moved into the main house, which meant he and Jonathan were a real couple, their commitment official. Milo's larger-than-life presence, his collection of offbeat artsy friends, turned Jonathan's home upside down. If Jonathan minded the commotion, he hadn't mentioned it. Kit loved having Milo around. She fancied being part of a hip bohemian artist's enclave—beyond cool. Writing again, living in a vibrant city, reconnecting with two of her favorite companions on earth, she sensed her ship had finally come.

An hour later, Kit's eye fell to the blank page, limp and curling in her word processor. To quit daydreaming and get back to work, she would need more caffeine. She smoothed her hair, zipped up her sweatshirt, grabbed her cup, and clomped up to the house for a refill. Bumping the door open with her hip, she lumbered in and found Jonathan at the kitchen table, head bent over the front page.

"Hey," she said quietly—her attempt to be cordial and noninvasive at the same time.

Jonathan mumbled a vague, distracted hello but did not look up from his paper.

Kit tiptoed to the pot and poured as subtly as possible.

Jonathan folded the newspaper and set it down. "How's the work going today?" he asked.

As she approached him, her eye caught the headline: *Iran Hostage Crisis Ends, 52 Released*. "It's going okay," she hedged.

Jonathan gave her a skeptical look, but before he could probe any further, Milo sashayed in.

Kit thought he looked like an oversized kid in his flannel pajamas. "Did you just wake up?"

"No, I've been glued to the tube all morning. Come see."

Kit took a hard look at Milo. His shoulders drooped and his complexion looked ashen. He'd caught some bug and was having trouble shaking it, thus hadn't been his effervescent self lately. She didn't mention it. "See what?" she asked.

Milo smirked. "It's fucking Reagan. He's being sworn in."

The three of them gathered in the TV room as the inauguration festivities began to unfold. The camera panned the crowd, then zeroed in on Nancy, first lady elect. Wearing a smart red suit and a frozen smile, she waved like a beauty queen.

Jonathan sank into the couch, unleashing a weary exhale. "If nothing else, it will be an interesting ride."

Kit squeezed in next to Jonathan as a ripple of trepidation rolled over her. She knew of Reagan's policies as governor of California. He'd opposed a woman's right to an abortion while supporting capital punishment. He'd called in the National Guard to quell protesters in Berkeley. His infamous quote, "If you've seen one redwood, you've seen them all," rang in her ears.

Kit sensed the ground beneath her shifting, and not in a good way. What would Reagan's presidency mean for their changing, troubled nation? Like riding a faulty carnival roller coaster, once it started rolling, there would be no getting off. They would have to ride it out.

She heard a tap at the front door. When neither man showed any sign of getting up, she rose to her feet. "Allow me, boys," she said with exaggerated ennui.

Kit appraised the door with a New Yorker's sensibility, checking the peephole first. Squinting at the good-looking guy on the porch, she gradually realized it was Ben, the mechanic who'd repaired her rental car a month ago. He wore a dark leather jacket and faded jeans—not too shabby sans the greasy coveralls. For unknown reasons, Kit's armpits prickled; her heart machine-gunned.

She slowly drew the door open. "Hi," she said, her voice too squeaky.

Ben dug his hands into his jacket pockets. "Hello, Kathrine," he said matter-of-factly.

Until now, she'd never noticed his eyes. They were awfully blue. "Everyone calls me Kit."

"Like Kit Carson?" he said, those blue eyes smiling.

Kit frowned. "I guess." After a long beat, she continued. "May I ask what you're doing here?"

"Sorry, I know it's kind of random, but I think I might have something you could use."

"Oh," she said, her confusion snowballing. "But how did you find me?"

His face went deadpan. "Hired a private detective."

Kit's cheeks burned. "You what?"

He held her in his gaze for a long moment then smiled slyly. "Just kidding. Nothing nefarious. I found you because you happened to write this address on the work order."

"Oh. Duh," she said. Kit vaguely recalled signing off on paperwork for the used bumper. "Sorry, but that doesn't explain why you're here."

Ben pointed down to the street. "What do you think?"

Kit glanced to the sidewalk, the houses, and the street below. "About what?"

Ben grinned at her. "Let me start over. Katherine, a customer of mine abandoned an old beat-up VW Bug in the shop. Anyway, I've been tinkering with it, and it runs decent now. Burns oil. I don't know, I guess I thought of you." He shrugged. "Maybe you could use it?"

Still baffled, Kit gawked at a reddish-brown Beetle, its tires wedged against the sidewalk. Pitiful and dented, with a lousy paint job, it was adorable. "You thought what?"

Ben looked dejected. "Yeah, I mean, only if you want it."

For a smart woman, Kit could be pretty dense. She finally put the pieces together. "Cool. How much do you want for it?"

He studied his sneakers. "I wouldn't charge you for that hunk of junk."

Like many New Yorkers, Kit had sworn off driving years ago, but she was in California now. Here *everyone* drove. She admitted a car would make her life easier; she was awfully tired of busses. She glanced back at the little car, her mind racing with possibilities. A car would allow her to see her dad more often, and God forbid, if he took another bad turn, she could be there within the hour. And she'd been pining to drive up the coast to revisit her old Humboldt stomping grounds. Still, Kit shook her head. "No way. I couldn't accept it."

Ben's face sobered. "Suit yourself," he said. An awkward silence ensued, then he grinned. "Tell you what, *Airplane* is playing at the Strand. You buy the tickets and popcorn, and we'll call it even."

Kit studied Ben, debating. If he'd wanted to ask her out, he certainly could have called. She really didn't know a thing about him. He could be an ax murderer, for all she knew. On the other hand, he was pretty cute. If nothing else, she had to give him points for originality. "Deal," she said.

San Francisco
Later That Week

The ringing phone wrenched Jonathan from the depths of sleep, the halo of a rather compelling dream lingering out of reach. In that hazy moment, the dream struck him as significant, yet he couldn't make out any specifics, only disjointed threads. He pried open his eyes to confront the glowing digital clock. His brain snapped awake, jumping to the worst case—Dylan? In danger, sick, or hurt?

Hell-bent on outrunning the jangling phone, he stumbled over Milo's sneakers, cursed all the way to the kitchen. He picked up the receiver, clutching it like a drowning man with a life preserver. "Kara?" He heard rustling, clatter, perhaps footsteps in the background. "Kara? Hello?" he said, raising his voice. "Is that you?"

"Wakefield?"

Jonathan's stomach bottomed out. "Yes, this is Jonathan Wakefield. Who's this?" But even as he voiced the question, he knew the answer. "Zimmerman?"

"Bingo."

His fist clenched. "Why the hell are you calling me at…" He checked the clock. "Five fifteen in the goddamn morning?"

109

Art chuckled as if he'd made an endearing faux pas. "Shit, sorry about that. I guess I'm upside down on time. You know how it is. Just got into Heathrow last night."

The mogul couldn't calculate simple time zones? Bullshit. Even Dylan could do that.

Art continued. "Look, I'm going to get right to the point."

"Yeah," Jonathan snapped.

"I need that draft, yesterday."

Jonathan twirled the phone cord, stretching it out, letting it retract. The January 1 deadline had come and gone, but his draft wasn't even close. He had no excuses, couldn't fault anyone but himself. "Art, I'm going to level with you." He took a deep breath and summoned the courage for confession. "I'm behind schedule."

"How close are you?"

"Pretty close." In truth, he'd been in the weeds for a while, couldn't bushwhack his way back to solid ground or envision any pathway leading to a proper end. The trail, he feared, had gone cold.

Art groaned. "Christ, Wakefield, I can't keep going to bat for you." He cleared his throat loudly, repeatedly. "Look, can you at least overnight me what you have? I have to show Marty something."

Jonathan pictured his opening chapters, solidly in place. He'd developed a believable protagonist, a gay man in his mid-thirties, a timely, politically charged setting—San Francisco. "Deal," Jonathan said. He supposed he owed Art that much. "But Art, I need you to renegotiate the deadline. I'll need at least six months."

"I can try to stall him, but no guarantees."

"Understood."

Jonathan replaced the phone and that moment pledged to get on with it. He brewed a pot, showered, dressed, and shut himself in his office, all before six o'clock. In the quiet of early morning, at least he could hear himself think. Then and there he vowed to attack the manuscript with gritty resolve. But soon, fragments of his dream crept in to invade his thoughts. The details remained hazy, but the dream had left an impression, perhaps a premonition, he couldn't shake.

His universe was about to be rocked, as if by some cataclysmic event, and it had something to do with Milo. Or maybe it had simply been a dream.

Regardless, he had to acknowledge that Milo's presence had energized and reanimated his life, opening doors to a brighter, fuller mélange of emotions. Milo's love had given his life new meaning and purpose, but his presence had also been a major distraction. He admitted he'd given into the trappings of sweet honeymoon sloth. Why coax recalcitrant words into useless sentences when he could be lollygagging in bed with his beloved?

He tapped his pen on the desktop, bringing himself back to the present. If this novel was ever going to see the light of day, he would need to forgo a bit of bliss. Yes, he'd have to set some boundaries, talk with Milo and Katherine, explain it to Dylan, too. He rather liked the idea of buckling down, conjuring his inner foreman, the orderliness and self-discipline he'd lacked.

Later that day, Jonathan carried a roast beef sandwich and a large cup of black coffee back to his office. He'd been at it all morning, intent on finishing the next chapter. Sinking into his chair, he took a bite of his sandwich, a sip of coffee, then turned his gaze to the page. He reread his last paragraph, debating. Shit or pure gold? He couldn't tell. He massaged the stubble on his chin, staring at the arrangement of black characters on white paper until his eyes crossed. Outside his tiny window, he noticed a light rainfall settling over the city, arguably the ideal climate for writing. Conditions were optimal—excuses nil.

But Jonathan continued to stare into nothingness, clicking his pen absently. Everything he'd ever wanted had fallen into place. His son was thriving, evolving, excelling, making friends. And dear Katherine—he'd never seen her happier. Milo, jazzed about his upcoming spring showcase—top secret, to be saved for the unveiling—had never been more engaged with his art. He counted himself lucky to reside with those he cherished in an atmosphere of passion and creativity. Who on earth could ask for more? All the arrows lined up, pointing to success.

Jonathan quit clicking his pen. He scratched out line after line, the blue ink, a blood stain. Then he crumpled the page and tossed it to the bin.

Downtown San Francisco
A Few Weeks Later
Saturday, February 14, 1981

As Kit nudged her bug into an absurdly tight spot, a few raindrops scattered on her windshield. She fed the meter then hurried across the street, ducking into the garage moments before a sudden cloudburst. The sharp scents of steel, petroleum, and mildew hung pleasantly in the air, smells she'd come to associate with Ben. She found him in the office. He sat close to a rattling space heater, its element glowing orange, so engrossed in his reading he didn't notice her arrival. With his head bent over a medical text, his long dark hair fell like a curtain around his face. She paused to admire the view.

"Hey, you," she said, giving him a little push.

He glanced up, looking startled. "Hey," he said. "Aren't you a little early?" He checked his watch. "Arlo's not due for twenty-five minutes."

Kit liked Arlo, Ben's long-time friend and fellow mechanic, but sometimes she wished he wasn't so punctual. "Sorry. I guess I missed you."

Ben gave her a wicked grin. "You missed me, huh?"

Despite the hulking counter between them, he managed to wrap his arms around her shoulders, pulling her close. Kit's eyes fell to the wiry strands of hair at the V of his collar. As their mouths met, she breathed in his scent, a dizzying meld of pheromones, flannel, and lime aftershave—undiluted masculinity. Kit resisted the urge to run her hands under his shirt. If not for Arlo's punctuality, she would have gone for it. Her lips grazed his, then lingered for another delicious interlude.

She backed away, collecting her wits. "How's the studying going?"

Ben's expression sobered. "It's going."

A pang of guilt shot to the pit of her stomach. What the hell was she thinking, showing up early? Ben's studies were crucial, his time limited, her presence a major distraction. If he flunked, it would be all her fault.

Well, maybe not entirely her fault.

Kit hadn't been looking for love, like the unexpected tabby that slipped through Jonathan's kitchen door last night. They weren't looking for a new pet, but the universe had other ideas. On the fateful day Ben appeared on Kit's doorstep, car keys in hand, he'd been the last person on earth she expected to see. Sure, she liked him, sort of, though he didn't strike her as boyfriend material. His courtship caught her off guard; she'd been unprepared for romance, not to mention the blistering attraction.

As each new piece of the Ben puzzle unfolded, her fondness grew. He'd honed his mechanical talent organically, working weekends and summers at the family Shell station. Motor oil ran through his veins, he'd quipped. His uncle and dad co-owned the place now since they didn't have the heart to sell it after Ben's granddad died. Ben still liked tinkering, as he called it, and pitched in when he could.

Kit would never forget her first impression of the "grease monkey" who happened to give her directions to the hospital, saving her ass. As she sat by her dad's bedside, watching him drift off to sleep, she thought she'd glimpsed Ben out of the corner of her eye. Kit had quickly dismissed the idea. A mechanic in scrubs? Next, fate arrived in the form of a AAA tow truck driver returning her to the Shell station. Ben fixed her car, saving her ass again, but never mentioned his true calling, medicine. Her gaze dropped to his textbook, propped open. Her stomach tightened. "You know, we can go hiking anytime."

Ben glowered at the book. "I don't know."

Kit met his eyes. "It's pouring out there. Let's do it another time."

He nodded, resigned. "I probably should go to the library."

The thought of leaving him physically pained her, but she forced a smile. "Yeah, good idea."

Ben ambled around the counter, taking her in his arms. "But it's your birthday."

Kit rested her head on his shoulder. "No biggie. We'll see each other tonight," she said, aware of the heat between them.

Arlo poked his head into the office. "Hey, man," he said. "You know, you can fix that noisy heater with a small nail."

Kit took in his bright, clean coveralls, the Giants cap askew. "Hi, Arlo," she said, not letting go of Ben. "Give us a second?"

Arlo got the message. "Shit, sorry to interrupt," he mumbled, backing out the door.

Ben's teeth grazed Kit's earlobe. "You're sure?"

Kit shivered. "I'm sure," she said, playfully shoving him away. "Now get back to work, buster."

***

Kit tore herself from Ben's warm hug and headed to her car all saintly and martyred, unsheltered from the drizzle. As she dashed across the street, she lost her footing. She attempted an ungainly shuffle before landing hard on her ass. Climbing unsteadily to her feet, she inventoried her injuries: torn jeans and damaged pride.

Returning home, she found no welcoming coffee pot, no waffles, no little Dylan to dazzle her with a violin solo, to wow her with his latest Lego creation. What had she been expecting? Candles and presents?

Today might be the anniversary of her birth, but it was also a Saturday, just like any other. She envisioned Jonathan and Dylan visiting the dinosaur exhibit at the Natural History Museum, or perhaps exploring Golden Gate Park. And Milo she pictured Saturday-hibernating. Knowing him, he wouldn't surface for hours.

Glumly, she settled in at the kitchen nook. Glancing at the newspaper headline, "Reagan to Announce Economic Recovery Plan," Kit's jaw set. She reached for a small pile of mail and began sorting it when the little uninvited, as-yet-unnamed houseguest appeared at her ankles.

Kit scooped up the kitten. "Hey, you."

The cat launched itself from her lap, landing feet first on the mail pile. Making a game of it, it swiped at envelopes and fliers, finally pouncing on Jonathan's unread paper.

Again, Kit corralled the kitten, this time holding it close to her body. "You're a feisty one, aren't you?"

The cat gazed innocently into Kit's eyes as if to say, *Me?*

She held the cat at arm's length, exposing its soft tummy and visually confirming its sex—male. Kit couldn't believe Dylan still hadn't decided on a name for the cute little fellow. "What should we call you, you handsome little interloper?"

She gave his head a scratch. He arched his back in pleasure, snaking closer for more. As she stroked his little body, he burrowed into the crook of her elbow, his quiet, calming purr melting her heart. She'd always loved animals. Even as a very young child, she'd pleaded for a warm, mammalian companion. Her father had been easy to convince, but her mother, averse to "the mess," summarily nixed the idea.

On her eighth birthday, she'd received the best gift ever—permission to pick any pet she wanted. All the way to the shelter, Kit's excitement bubbled and fizzed. But upon encountering rows of concrete animal cages, her stomach had twisted with anguish. She hadn't been prepared for the sharp odor of fear, the heartbreaking lineup of tragic souls in need of simple human kindness. Her own mother had disappeared less than a year earlier, and in the eyes of every dog she saw the scars of desertion. Unable to save them all, she'd chosen Charlie, a sturdy little white mutt with brown spots. Thinking back, she acknowledged it had been he who rescued her, not vice versa.

The cat yawned, repositioning himself in Kit's lap. She returned her attention to sorting the mail and discovered a square blue envelope addressed to her. Kit clutched it, taking in the left-leaning script, both loopy and squished, her stomach swimmy. Her dad, unwittingly, must have divulged her new address. While he'd long since forgiven her for leaving, Kit still held a righteous grudge.

Hit with a déjà vu-ish creeping sensation like someone was watching her, she glanced up, instantly spotting the culprit—Milo.

He hovered in the doorway wearing a black silk kimono and a sleepy, puzzled expression. "Hey, valentine slash birthday girl. I thought you were supposed to be trekking up some mountain with your new sweetheart."

As if spooked, the kitten bolted. Kit discreetly poked the envelope to the bottom of the pile. "Rained out," she said. "How long have you been standing there?"

He yawned. "Long enough."

Kit gave him the once-over. "Nice threads."

Milo did a super-gay exaggerated twirl. "Do you like it?"

"Very much."

"An early birthday present from Jon," he said. Then, as if to include her, he added, "my fellow Aquarian."

Kit met his eyes. "Aquarians forever."

Milo sat next to her—so close he was practically in her lap. He plucked the blue envelope from the bottom of the stack. "From your mom?"

Milo's ability to read Kit bordered on the supernatural, and sometimes— like now—she wished he'd give it a rest. She also wished her mom would quit sending meaningless cards—and hoped she would never quit. Fuck.

"Were you going to open it?" he nudged.

"I suppose," Kit said, a bitter edge in her voice. "I just wish it didn't get to me."

Milo draped an arm around her. "I know."

Kit tensed, doubled down on her anger. But the more she dug in, the more fragile she felt, her will an eggshell. Surrendering, she allowed her head to rest on Milo's chest, his arm snug around her shoulder.

Every year her mother's birthday box arrived like clockwork. First had come the unwanted Barbies, the Hershey bars. Then the ill-fitting jeans and too-young books. Even as a child, Kit had been dubious about her mom's offerings. Presents didn't compensate for a mother's absence; they underscored the void. Sure, her mom never forgot a birthday, but how hard was it to remember

February 14? Eventually the boxes tapered off, replaced by a safer bet. A card —
a check.

Kit handed the envelope to Milo. "You open it," she said flatly.

Milo studied the envelope. "Are you sure?"

"I'm sure."

"As you wish," Milo said. He tore open the envelope and removed the
Peanuts-themed card. "Cute," he said.

"Read it," Kit said.

Milo opened the card and, predictably, discovered the folded check inside.
"How much?" Kit asked.

As Milo unfolded the check, his eyes nearly popped out of his head. "Kit-
Kat, you're rich."

Kit snatched the check from his hand. "Five hundred bucks," she said.
"That's ten times what I expected."

He treated her to a luminous grin. "Well, I guess it kind of makes up for
all the shitty stuff, right?"

Kit choked out a laugh. "It's a start."

San Francisco
A Few Weeks Later

Monday rolled in, bringing a soggy blanket of San Francisco fog. His morning coffee on board, Jonathan showered, dressed, and steeled himself for a productive day, hell or high water. With Dylan in school and Milo ensconced at the gallery, he couldn't justify a valid rationale to postpone. February had come and gone. Time was ticking, and he'd run out of excuses. He resolved to break only for the call of nature, restless limbs, or growling stomach.

But as he entered his office and shut the door behind him, yet again, a vague twitchy dread came over him. He glanced down to his desk, his unfinished novel a slim stack of white pages. Sweat beaded above his upper lip, his brow. To tackle his manuscript without a second cup of coffee, maybe a slice of toast, would be ill-advised, he reasoned.

Jonathan's rationalizations had become more fluid and frequent of late, but for now, he shoved that troubling thought underground and made his way to the kitchen. To his delight, he discovered Katherine at the griddle flipping pancakes.

She noticed him come in and her expression brightened. "What a nice surprise," she said. "It's been a while."

Since she'd started seeing Ben, Katherine certainly smiled a lot more often, drunk on endorphins no doubt. He recognized her symptoms, as he, too, buzzed with the electricity of early-stage amour. "I know, it feels like ages."

She nodded. "I guess we've both been pretty busy."

"Two ships . . . " he said.

She looked pretty, her skin aglow in the pale morning light. Dressed like a hippy in faded jeans and a muslin peasant blouse, she wore her hair gathered in a loose bun. A far cry from the sheepish, bookish girl he'd met in Humboldt, Katherine Hilliard had blossomed.

Katherine poured more batter onto the griddle. "Would you like some pancakes?"

Taking a good look at the platter of golden-brown stack he concluded they were precisely the diversion he needed. "Yes, please," he said. "Do you need any help?"

"I've got it," she said.

Jonathan settled in at the nook. He scanned yet another dismal story about Reagan's economic endeavors, eyeing Kit as she loaded their plates. "My God, you've made enough for a small army."

"Old habits die hard. Ever since my Waffle Hamlet days, I can never make just a few," she quipped. She placed a plate in front of him, then one for herself. With a waitress's practiced dexterity, she arranged forks, napkins, butter, jam, and syrup. "Voila."

As he took in the feast before him, his stomach grumbled. "Looks delicious."

"Coffee?"

"I'll get it," he said as he leapt to his feet.

Katherine waved him off. "Let me. It's time I fed you for a change."

The aroma of pancakes—notes of maple sugar, freshly baked bread, cake—evoked the mouthwatering scents of the neighborhood bakery. He picked up his fork but resisted taking a bite.

"Dig in," Katherine said, setting their coffee cups on the table.

He drizzled a bit of syrup on top and watched it drip down the stack, provocative as Mrs. Butterworth's commercial. At last, he tucked into the delicate cakes. "Outstanding."

Katherine raised an eyebrow. "At least I have one marketable skill. If this writing thing doesn't pan out, I can always work at IHOP."

"Unlike me," he said, his gloom unhidden.

Katherine gave him a hard look. She set her fork on her plate. "Not going so well?"

"Totally stalled," he admitted. "My snake of an agent is on my ass, my publisher's giving me ultimatums, but I'm stuck—can't seem to move forward." He'd been holding it in for so long, he hadn't meant to let it slip. In the strained silence that followed, Jonathan lost his appetite. He frowned at his cup. "Sorry," he said. "I shouldn't dump my problems on you."

Her brow furrowed. "Please, don't say that." She squeezed his hand. "I hope you know you can always confide in me."

"I appreciate your support," he said. Disquieting role reversal aside, he had to concede his confession had helped to loosen the knot in his gut, giving him a measure of relief. "It's good to get it off my chest."

"If it's any consolation, I know how you feel."

"When did you become so wise, Ms. Hilliard?"

She met his eyes. "I had a wise teacher. He taught me that struggle was inevitable, an integral part of the process. He taught me to be brave, trust my instincts—you know, stick with it."

Ah, the irony. His own words coming back to bite him in the ass. "I can't argue with that." He took a deep breath. "Now, let's talk about you. How was your birthday?"

"Nice," she said. She thought it over. "Different," she amended.

"How so?"

She drenched her pancakes with syrup, emptying the tiny pitcher. "For one thing, this year I got to see my parents."

"What's your hesitation?"

"I suppose I've always regarded Cindy as separate—my dad's wife—but lately she feels more like my mom."

121

Jonathan recalled his brief encounters with Katherine's folks, the first time at her graduation, then a few years later in New York at her book launch. They'd struck him as solid salt-of-the earth types, the kind of parents he wished he'd had. "Glad to hear you're feeling close to her," he said. "How's your dad's health?"

"He's much better, almost back to normal."

"Wonderful," Jonathan said.

"He's become a real health nut, even joined the Y. But that's good, right?"

"Definitely. Where did you go for dinner?"

"They wanted to do all the touristy stuff, so we ate dinner in Chinatown. It was good," she said, smiling at the fond memory. "Ben met us at the restaurant."

Jonathan grinned. Thanks to Milo, he considered himself a bit of a romance expert these days. For the first time in his wretched life, he understood the meaning of love. It wasn't the grand gestures, but all the small things— simple smile or unexpected kindness. "Did Ben pass muster?"

Katherine shrugged. "Pretty sure Dad approved."

"And what about you? Do you approve?"

Her face colored. "Ben is the perfect man, really. He's generous, thoughtful, intelligent, driven, ambitious, and damn good-looking."

"But?"

She grimaced slightly. "I don't know. It all happened so fast."

"Too fast?"

"Whirlwind. The thing is, when we started hanging out, he was on break. But now he's crazy busy with his medical internship and studies, so he rarely has time for any social life. When we do get together, it feels like he's watching the clock."

Jonathan scratched his chin, thinking. "But are you compatible? You respect him as a person?" he probed.

She looked down. "I think I might love him. Or maybe, I think I ought to love him."

He studied her as she contemplated her plate, but was unable to read her, uncertain what to say next. "Sounds difficult," he said. It was all he had.

She picked up her fork, pushed her food around the plate. "I think I'll survive," she said, one eyebrow raised. "Now it's my turn to change the subject."

"Fair enough."

"Have you seen the wind chimes Milo made for me?"

Indeed, he'd seen them. He'd found them quite remarkable, a departure from Milo's bulkier works. "I take it you like them?"

Katherine's expression brightened. "He's so talented. I don't know how he managed to create something so delicate, exquisite, and clever out of junk. The way he embedded the driftwood with sea glass and twisted the forks and spoons." She grinned. "Seriously, he blows my mind."

He nodded. "The silverware, a symbol of your time together at Waffle Hamlet, right?"

"Yes, he really touched my heart." She shook her head. "That loveable goofball."

A tiny shiver shot through Jonathan. He, too, loved that goofball. Milo's love had freed him to laugh with abandon, to sob openly, to melt into another. God help him. He loved him so much it made him ache, even scared him a little. Scared him a lot. "By the way, I have something for you as well."

"My goodness, I'm intrigued."

"Stay put. I'll be right back."

He'd spotted the perfect gift a month ago and stowed it away for safekeeping in the drawer of his antique phone table. As he retrieved it, he happened upon a note in Dylan's handwriting. He shoved the scrap of paper into his pocket.

"Happy late birthday," he said, aware of his glaringly book-shaped present.

"I wonder what it could be," she joked. She peeled away the tape, taking care not to rip the paper as she unveiled the book. "*East of Eden*. My God, it's perfect," she said, running her hand along the worn spine. As she opened the book, her eyes widened. "A first edition? Oh, Jonathan, thank you."

"You like it?"

123

She stood and gave him a fierce hug. "You know I do," she said. "I love it."

He held her close, nearly moved to tears himself. "You're very welcome."

Katherine released him. "I'd better clean up this mess and get back to work. My word processor is calling."

"I'll clean up. You get to it. He patted his pocket. "Oh, I almost forgot," he said.

He dug into his pocket, fishing out the slip of paper. "Dylan took a phone message for you."

Katherine unfolded the note. As she read it, her eyes narrowed. She seemed to forget Jonathan's presence altogether, then made a hasty, silent exit.

He wondered. Was she angry, elated, scared? The only thing he knew for certain—the power of words. In this case, two syllables rendered in his child's familiar script.

Joe called.

Moments Later

Kit thundered down the steps, bulldozed into the studio, closed the door, and confronted the paper scrap, crushed and damp in her palm. *Joe called. Joe called.* Glaring at the cryptic loaded message, her emotions bounced around like a Super Ball in a tight space, from the painful clot of sadness in her throat to the quiet thrill of possibility aflutter in her chest. The Super Ball landed in the floor of her belly. Her mind raced; her breath rose and fell in shallow snatches. Was she hyperventilating? Out of nowhere, a hauntingly beautiful melody drifted on the edge of her awareness. Kit threw the door open and took a gulp of air. She turned her gaze to the eaves, where she spotted Milo's wind chimes dancing. When had he found the time to hang them up for her? And true to form, he'd chosen the optimal spot to catch the afternoon breeze. As she admired his thoughtfulness, his creativity, the wind began to play. The slightest breeze animated the chimes with percussive tones like a spectrum of colors. Bright high notes blended with low gong-like beats. The music resonated in Kit's body, quieting her mind—reminding her to lighten the hell up. She smiled, despite herself.

What would Milo say if he could see her now? He'd admonish her, she knew, to get a grip. *Why fret over a phone call? A blip in the greater cosmic scheme.* And he would be right. The mere thought of Joe had sent her reeling, and not for the first time. Kit frowned at the washed-out sky, her analytical wheels

125

turning, curiosity awakened. Why? After so many years, why did he still get to her?

She returned inside, took a seat at her little desk, and rummaged through the drawer for a pen and notepad. As if possessed, she began writing.

I Saw You

She continued jotting rapidly, without thinking or judgment.

Shirtless
Brown skin aglow
Long dark hair, tangled and dripping from the shower
Red towel loose around your shoulders, nonchalant
A tiny forest of chest hair funneling to a sparse line down your belly
The button fly of those goddamn faded Levi's, a suggestion
Fatal

She put her pen down and sat with the memory for a while. The well-worn impression of her first encounter with Joe was etched in her mind. Countless times she'd relived the moment, unblemished by time.

Kit thought better on her feet. She stood and began pacing the floor, piecing the past together like a complicated jigsaw. Joe had been her first love, she acknowledged. More to the point, she admitted, her first heart-pounding, spine-tingling, off-the charts orgasm. In the sex department, her experience was limited. Freshman year she'd had a long-term boyfriend, David, but the sex had felt detached. She'd gone through the motions but never got out of her head. After they broke up, there had been a couple other guys, but no one exceptional.

Joe changed everything. The way he never rushed but lingered. His fingertips caressing her cheek, her lips; Joe met her gaze, drinking her in as if she were some goddess. When they kissed, it felt like drowning. Hours disintegrated. That first week, they'd lived in bed, spellbound in their own private, steamy universe. The outside world with its complications simply paled. Remembering, Kit sat down on the edge of her bed, her expression faraway. The attraction had been predestined, irresistible. An origin story she'd told and retold.

Then it hit her. There had been many dark days before Joe arrived on the scene. Her eyes pricked with tears as the memories surfaced. Her classmates and teachers, her roommate JJ, and even Milo had split from Arcata, leaving Kit to dwell on her regrettable actions. Her worries had magnified, tying knots of shame and dread she couldn't untangle. On the heels of that grim, drizzly three-week Christmas vacation, Kit had never felt more alone.

Her saga began—and ended—with Jonathan. She still flushed with embarrassment when she recalled her infatuation with her handsome, brilliant teacher, her misguided belief that Jonathan had desired her, too.

Dominos lined up.

One: Kit invites Jonathan to a dinner party, hoping to impress him.

Two: Milo brings magic mushrooms, which everyone including Jonathan gobbles. Kit declines—natch.

Three: Erin, her supposed friend, seduces Jonathan in Kit's own fucking bedroom, then goes home with him.

Four: She discovers Jonathan hadn't been with Erin, but her best friend, Milo. Poor, dopey, naïve, deluded Kit. It never even occurred to her that her best guy friend was gay.

Dominos fell.

Something inside of her broke, as if her entire worldview had been a fantasy—a joke. Blinded by confusion, scorn, beer, marijuana, and righteous poor judgment, she'd wanted to lash out, to punish Jonathan for his betrayal, for breaking her heart.

Blowing off her final exam, she'd enlisted Erin to roll joints and help her plot Jonathan's demise. Crafting a damning letter to the dean, they outed Jonathan. From the moment Erin slipped it into the mailbox, Kit had been overcome with regret. Even now, shame coursed through her veins, her blood. Jonathan had long since forgiven her, but she would never forgive herself.

Kit remembered back to the sinking feeling, how she knew Christmas vacation would soon end. The lonely, dreadful weeks had been bad, but things were bound to get worse. Students would repopulate Arcata. JJ would return. Monday morning the dean would read her letter. Kit had dug a hole of misery with no apparent way out.

Enter Joe.

On the weekend before spring quarter, Joe's timely appearance had marked the end of Kit's isolation. She pictured their chance meeting for the zillionth time. Had he been a convenient distraction from her woes? Kit plugged in the single-burner hot plate, a birthday gift from Dad and Cindy. She dumped a packet of hot chocolate, also from her parents, into a cup. In retrospect, she realized Joe's laser beam of attention had saved her, but the whirlwind had been short-lived. Less than six months later, when the relationship had taken a more serious turn, Kit headed off to New York, leaving a trail of promises in her wake. *I will always love you. I will come back to you. I will marry you.*

Too impatient to let the water boil, Kit poured warm water into her cup, stirring the chocolate mixture with her index finger. Did she regret her choice? At the time, her prospects had been promising—nothing but green pastures for miles. Deep down, she'd wanted to make Jonathan proud, to become the Katherine he believed in. She owed him that. If her life had turned out differently, would she have given Joe a second thought?

Kit carried her cup to her desk and picked up her pen again. As she reached for her notepad, she glanced over at her nightstand to the phone, daring her to pick up the receiver.

About Two Weeks Later

Jonathan peeked into Dylan's bedroom to catch him quietly toiling on his social studies project. Dylan knelt on the rug, deep in concentration, an empty cereal bowl by his side. Jonathan suspected the kid had been at it since daybreak. "How's it going?"

Dylan looked up as if awoken from a pleasant dream. "Okay."

Jonathan admired his son's determination. Tasked with creating a scale model of a Spanish mission, *the* iconic California assignment, even in a progressive Waldorf school, Dylan had fully embraced the challenge. After much deliberation, he decided to tackle Mission San Juan Bautista, situated in a quaint, dusty village about two hours south of San Francisco.

They'd visited the mission last weekend for inspiration. Jonathan had been struck by the town's California character, so unlike Minnesota. Clay-colored adobe dwellings vined with red bougainvillea, chickens roaming the streets, the dusty El Camino Real, a tranquility belying its bloody history. As they toured the mission, Jonathan had allowed Dylan to take his time, snapping photos, deliberating over trinkets from the gift shop. They'd had cheese enchiladas and chips on a lovely outdoor patio before heading back to the city.

Jonathan sat cross-legged on the floor, evaluating Dylan's progress. "Looking good, kiddo."

129

Dylan turned to his dad. "I need more red," he said, his brow knitted. "For the roof."

"Okay," Jonathan said, happy to serve as his assistant. He began sorting through a large green tub filled with Dylan's chosen medium, Legos. "I'll look for red."

Dylan nodded.

With a faint smile, he recalled the day Dylan had announced his assignment. The kid did not procrastinate. He immediately began sorting his Legos by color and size, and when his collection proved deficient, he'd asked for Jonathan's help. Trolling secondhand stores to supplement two key colors for the project, red and white, his search had yielded little. It had been Milo who hit the jackpot, cleaning out a used toy store in Lincoln Park. Dylan had taken to Milo from the start, but the Lego windfall sealed his acceptance.

A tubful of Legos? This, Jonathan could accomplish. In fact, he welcomed all distractions. Anything to avoid the misery of his ongoing failure, his deadline looming, his novel flatlining. Intent on the task at hand, he failed to notice the cat sidle in to pounce and scatter his newly sorted bricks.

"Hey, you," he said, grabbing the cat, corralling him on his lap. The cat squirmed out of Jonathan's grasp in a kinetic frenzy, batting at his red Lego prey.

Dylan collapsed into a giggle fit. "Crazy kitty."

Jonathan managed to intercept the little rascal, holding him at arm's length. "Listen, you," he said. "Mission San Juan Bautista is off-limits."

Dylan knelt by his dad's side, stroking the cat's sleek fur.

Kitty yawned and nestled into Jonathan's lap, apparently ready for a long nap. The soothing vibration of the feline purr lent a calming effect. "You know, we can't keep calling him *Kitty*. He's part of our family now. He deserves a name, don't you think?"

Dylan scratched the cat's head. "I agree."

"Have you decided?"

"Not yet."

Jonathan released an exaggerated, put-upon sigh. "I suppose I'll have to do it," he said. "I like Whiskers. That's a good, solid name, don't you think?"

Dylan grimaced. "No way."

"Fine. We'll call him Tiger."

"No!"

"Felix?"

Dylan waved the offending name off with a sweep of his hand. "That's terrible."

"Well, he's got nice, thick fur. How about Fluffy?"

The boy's expression sobered. "I like the name Zeke."

"Zeke? Like your friend from school?"

Dylan nodded.

Jonathan pretended to consider it. "It suits him," he concluded.

Zeke offered no opinion, so the name stuck.

Later that afternoon, Dylan emerged from his bedroom into the kitchen, tired but triumphant. "I'm almost finished with the mission. Can I watch TV now?"

"Sure," Jonathan said.

The boy skittered into the TV room to join Milo and Katherine. They'd recently taken to watching roller derby, a bizarre spectacle Jonathan didn't fully approve of for a ten-year-old kid. As he tidied the kitchen, he looked forward to a nice Sunday dinner. Still, a cloud hung in the air. Sunday evenings were always a little bittersweet, his time with Dylan dwindling. He sensed the weekend evaporating, gears grinding into Monday.

The phone rang, cutting through Jonathan's musings. When those engrossed in roller derby failed to get off the couch, he picked up.

"Jon?"

"Yes?"

"It's me."

Kara's voice sounded faraway with an otherworldly echo. His chest constricted. "Are you okay?"

She breathed heavily into the receiver. "We're stuck at SeaTac. Our flight was grounded. Looks like we have to spend the night."

He'd forgotten about Kara and Kent's Seattle trip. Jonathan respected his ex, even loved her in a fraternal way. But lately communication between them had been reduced to the business of co-parenting, with little overlap into each other's personal lives. Their marriage had faded into soft focus, with details he could no longer envision. "That's a drag," he said. "But better safe than sorry."

"You make a good point," she said wearily.

The purpose of Kara's travels dawned on him. She'd mentioned visiting Seattle to negotiate the acquisition of another gallery. "How did your meeting go?"

"Good. We still need to iron out a few details. I'll fill you in when we get back."

"Okay," he said, keeping his voice neutral as his mind raced. If they acquired a gallery in Seattle, she might consider relocating. Would they want to take Dylan? A small, grudging part of him envied Kara's wealth and professional acumen, the way she'd blossomed without him. Still, he owed her. If not for Kara, he never would have moved to San Francisco, back to Dylan. It had been Kara who'd recognized Milo's talent. She'd mentored him in the business of art.

"Jon? Are you still there?"

"Yes, I'm here. We must have a bad connection."

"So, can you take Dylan to school tomorrow?"

"Of course."

"Did he finish his mission?"

"Yes. He did an excellent job, really. He's so proud of it."

"Thanks to you, Jon," she said. "Can I talk to him?"

Jonathan called Dylan to the phone. TV-distracted, the boy repeated the word *okay* a few times, then *love you, too*, before hanging up. He turned to his dad. "Can we get Angelina's tonight?"

Jonathan had been craving Dylan's favorite pizza, loaded with pepperoni, mushrooms, and black olives. "Great minds think alike," he said, picking up the phone. The evening opened as the Sunday cloud lifted.

***

132

TV off, everyone gathered at the table for dinner. The fare, Angelina's pizza and family-sized green salad with chocolate ice cream for dessert, sublime. Jonathan couldn't help but notice Dylan's buoyant mood. He grinned and chatted all through dinner, hopped up on roller derby and pride in his accomplishment.

"I like the way you built your courtyard—very realistic," said Milo. "And I'll bet no one else used Legos."

Dylan nodded. "Thanks."

Milo continued. "I also bet a lot of parents did the work, but you did it on your own—that's impressive."

Katherine gave Milo a wink. "Looks like we have another artist in the family," she said.

Jonathan smiled. The word resonated. Indeed, they had become a family, perhaps a bit ragtag, but a family, nonetheless. He turned to Milo. "Speaking of art, that reminds me. How's your show coming?"

"It's coming," Milo said.

Katherine's expression brightened. "It's April 18, right?"

Milo nodded grimly.

"Maybe I'll invite Ben," Katherine said. "I can't wait. The suspense is killing me."

"You'll have to wait," Milo said gravely.

Milo looked tired. He'd been working too hard, refusing Jonathan's offers to help with the setup. Jonathan knew the stakes were high. Milo had never produced a solo show. Kara had been promoting him all month, and with her connections, Milo would receive international media coverage. Jonathan placed his hand on Milo's arm, giving him a loving, knowing look.

They lingered at the table, enjoying each other's company for a long while, until Jonathan glanced at his watch. "It's almost nine, son. Tomorrow's school. Time for pajamas and brushing teeth. I'll come check on you in a few minutes, okay?"

Dylan yawned. For once, he didn't argue.

After reading to Dylan and tucking him into bed, Jonathan went to clean up the kitchen, but someone had beaten him to it. The house lay still. He envisioned Katherine cozied in the studio, Milo waiting for him in bed. A sense of peace washed over him. Despite a case of debilitating writer's block, he'd never been happier.

Jonathan locked the front door and hit the light switch. He glanced out the window and spotted Beth, slumped on her stoop smoking a cigarette as the rain drizzled down her eaves. Her figure appeared frail in the unearthly glow of her porch light. She wore a sleeveless nightgown, leaving her exposed to the elements. Impulsively he grabbed one of his old Minnesotan sweaters from the hall closet.

As he crossed the street, he called her name, his voice muted by the rain. The din of distant traffic and the slap of his own feet on wet asphalt rang in his ears. When he arrived at her porch, he saw that she was shivering. "Beth?"

Beth recoiled like a cornered animal, then squinted at him. "Jonathan? What are you doing here?"

Bruise-colored half-moons beneath her eyes brought a painful lump to his throat. "I thought you might need this," he said, draping her birdlike shoulders with his bulky cardigan.

Her lower lip trembled. "Thanks." She stubbed out her cigarette, then reached into the pack for another. With the cig between her lips, she thumbed her lighter, but her hand was unsteady.

"Allow me," Jonathan said.

Beth frowned, dropping the lighter into his palm.

He flicked it, cupped the flame, and lit her cigarette, watching as she exhaled a cloud of bluish smoke into the rain. Though it had been years since he crushed his last box of Marlboros, his primitive brain reverted. The craving, a cavity in the pit of his stomach. "Mind if I bum one?"

Beth gave him a skeptical look but plucked one from her pack.

Jonathan took a tentative drag, the harsh smoke burning his lungs. The second drag came easier, the act of smoking apparently like riding a bike. He glanced at Beth's drawn, sallow face. "Is everything okay?" he asked lamely. Clearly everything was *not* okay.

"It's my baby," she said, barely above a whisper. "The hospital called— yesterday."

Jonathan recalled the harrowing night he'd driven Beth to the hospital, her car out of commission. He pictured Jamie's gaunt shape beneath the thin hospital covers. "The hospital?"

Beth hung her head. "I thought he was getting better."

The bottom fell out of Jonathan's stomach. "My God, what happened?" He tossed his cigarette to the wet ground, wrapped his arm around her. "He moved out recently, didn't he?"

Beth grimaced. "About a month ago. I wish he would have called me; you know?"

"Yes."

"He was in so much pain. Awful sores all on the soles of his feet, his legs. Doctor said it was some fast-growing. . . cancer."

He helped Beth inside. As he waited for her to change into dry clothes, he glanced around her tiny apartment with a voyeuristic eye. He'd half expected her place to be unkempt, like her, but despite the worn furnishings, it was clean and well ordered. Jonathan entered her galley kitchen, put the kettle on. Upon opening a cupboard, he found an unopened bottle of Jack Daniels amid the cereal boxes, sugar, coffee, and tea.

As he stood in her kitchen making her a hot cup of booze-fortified chamomile tea, he tried to put himself in Beth's shoes. He couldn't fathom the depths of her suffering, the financial and emotional toll, repeatedly trying and failing to rescue her heroin-addicted son. At nineteen, Jamie had run away from Tempe, Beth had said, hitchhiking all the way to San Francisco. She'd been frantic with worry.

Like so many young people, Jamie had fallen prey to the streets. Hitting bottom, he'd phoned Beth in the middle of the night frightened, broke, and alone. She didn't hesitate to upend her life, boarding a six-in-the-morning flight to San Francisco. She'd loved him with ferocity, bailing him out time and time again. The flowery yellowy scent of chamomile filled the air, making him slightly queasy. He realized he'd judged Beth for caving into Jamie's ceaseless requests for cash, but admitted that if it had been Dylan, he probably would have done the same.

Beth sunk into her purple crushed-velvet couch, Jonathan in the matching chair, the air thick with anguish. He handed her the tea and she took a sip. If she noticed the whiskey, she didn't mention it. "I met Stefan," she said, shaking her head in disbelief.

"Stefan?"

"At the hospital," she said, clutching her teacup with both hands. "His boyfriend." Her face fell. "I didn't even fucking know he was gay."

Jonathan returned to Beth's kitchen and located two juice glasses. He grabbed the bottle, sunk back into his chair, and poured each of them a shot. "Does it matter?"

Beth slumped. "No," she said. "I just wish he would have told me."

Poor kid. Jonathan knew all too well the oppression and tyranny of staying in the closet. He'd spent most of his life twisted up with shame, desperate to exorcise the gay, to pass for so-called normal. Though he'd made peace with his identity, scars remained. "He was probably scared."

For a long while, he simply sat with Beth in her sorrow, allowing the silence. He did not try to console her. The words did not exist.

Beth drank her whiskey in one pull. Held up her glass for another, then another.

Jonathan poured the last of the liquor from the bottle. "What about your family?" he asked, breaking the silence. ·

Beth nodded. "My brother and parents are on their way, flying in from Tempe. They're going to help me with the arrangements, to take Jamie's . . ." She took several shaky breaths. "Jamie's body back home."

Jonathan nodded.

"My parents want me to move home, stay with them for a while."

"What do you think?"

Beth gulped the shot, slammed the glass down on the table. "I hate this fucking town. I only came here for Jamie. No reason for me to stay." She yawned deeply. "Sorry, I haven't slept in two days." Stretching out on the couch, she rested her head on a pillow. In no time, sleep mercifully took her. Jonathan covered her with a throw blanket, and with a heavy heart let himself out.

Later That Week
Ten Miles South of Notley's Landing

As Kit steered her trusty VW Bug though a series of corkscrew turns on a remote stretch of Highway 1, her mind was elsewhere. When she'd told Ben about traveling to Big Sur to meet an *old friend* from college, leaving out the clarifier *boy*-friend, technically she hadn't lied to him—unless one counted lies of omission. Guilt rode alongside her, a specter, filling her head with confusion.

It would have been easier if Ben had been a jerk about it. But he didn't act possessive or probe Kit for details about said *friend*. In keeping with his Boy Scout nature, he'd checked her tires, replaced her spark plugs, and made her promise to drive safely. Ben's concern for her well-being magnified her shame. She couldn't deny the glaring irony. Trusting, generous Ben had given her a car, no strings attached. Now it had become a vehicle of betrayal.

Her thoughts circled back to the morning after her birthday. The dinner with Ben and her parents had gone better than expected—even her dad approved. Then Jonathan handed her a scrap of paper, upending everything. Kit spent the entire day reeling, debating with herself, tossing Joe's phone number into the trash, digging it out again. Only when the sun disappeared and night closed in, did she finally pick up the phone. She'd let it ring fifteen or sixteen times and had been seconds from chickening out when Joe finally picked up.

Kit downshifted, steering into an abrupt sharp turn. The road ahead snaked, hugging the craggy outcroppings above the endless Pacific, her tires perilously close to the edge. She failed to notice the jaw-dropping scenery, thinking only of Joe's out-of-breath voice when he'd answered the phone. *Kit?*

His naked hope brought a wave of shame. She'd laughed involuntarily, masking her emotions. "Yes, it's me."

Joe had also laughed. Then his tone sobered, as if paving the way for confession. He let out a long breath before speaking. "I've had kind of an epiphany."

Kit flopped down on the bed, stretching the phone cord to its limit. The knots in her shoulders released a little. "What do you mean, an epiphany?"

Joe went on to describe his experience as Kit closed her eyes, envisioning him. He'd been headed to the laundromat when he reached for a random cassette, blindly popping it into the player. The track "Tupelo Honey" played, tidal waving him with memories, stabbing him with a pain so sharp he'd had to pull over.

"That's when it hit me," he'd said.

"What?"

"The date. It was February 14, your birthday."

Kit imagined Joe capsized by the side of the road, a basket of laundry in the back seat, strains of "Tupelo Honey" stirring love and longing. The song triggered memories for her, too. The taste of chocolate frosting on her lips. Holding Joe close, swaying to Van Morrison, falling into bed. "Mm hm," she said, giving nothing away.

He'd let out a long exhale. "That's when I knew," he said, choking up. "I couldn't let you go, Kit. Not again."

As Kit digested Joe's words, the exact words she'd craved for years, her heart remained firmly closed. Why now? Did he think he could discard her, then wag his finger and expect her to come running? Her shoulders turned to cement. "Aren't you engaged to, what's her name? Melanie?" she'd asked all snarky.

"It's over," he'd said, flatly. "I broke it off with her."

A quiet thrill fluttered in Kit's chest, but she kept quiet.

Joe continued. "I know it may seem . . ."

Kit gathered her wits. Without skipping a beat, she cut him off. "The thing is, I have a new boyfriend." She paused, letting it sink in. "He's a doctor," she'd said with cool detachment. After dropping that bomb, she figured she'd never hear from Joe again.

It hadn't been a total lie, had it? Nothing had changed. Regardless of Joe's broken engagement, she'd moved on, hadn't she? She probably loved Ben. Certainly, she admired him. And why not? He was ambitious, open, easy to talk to, intelligent, compassionate. And, as she'd recently discovered, quite talented in bed.

The awareness of Ben's existence did not deter Joe. Rather, it seemed to spur him on. He began calling Kit often, late at night. She'd played it cool at first but found herself guiltily looking forward to the sound of the ringing phone. As February faded into March, Ben's demanding pre-med schedule left little time for Kit. She admitted that Joe's late-night calls filled a gap.

Joe had made it clear he wanted her back, but he never pressured her. They'd end up chatting for hours, catching up on the last five years, reminiscing about the old days, talking politics, bullshitting about nothing. Easy, meandering conversations. No thorny topics, such as feelings for each other. But late at night, alone in the dark, Kit let her guard down. Their growing closeness felt so right, so wrong, a little bit naughty.

On a chilly night in late March, pale moonlight streaming through Kit's window, Joe suggested meeting face-to-face.

"I want to see you, Kit," he'd said. "Let me treat you to a birthday brunch."

She'd chuckled. "But my birthday was over a month ago."

"Belated birthday, then," Joe offered.

Without hesitation, Kit had accepted his invitation, even as a little voice in her head whispered, *What about Ben?*

A brown streak shot across the road—a squirrel? Kit snapped back to the present, braking hard and swerving onto the gravel shoulder. Taking a sharp, shallow breath, she glanced into her rearview mirror. She checked the road ahead—all clear. Shit, that was close. Gathering her wits, she inched back to the road, where she spotted an artsy sign in bold yellow Greco-Roman script:

Nepenthe. The word conjured her favorite class senior year, etymology. If memory served, the derivation would likely be Greek, *Ne* (not) and *Penthos* (grief or pain). No pain. Trippy.

Kit arrived about thirty minutes early, pleased with her slight "home court advantage"—lead time to collect her wits and assess the layout before Joe showed up. Entering Nepenthe, like stepping back in time, the restaurant filled her with unsettling déjà-vu. As her gaze traveled to the open-beam ceilings, the woodsy, hippy vibe, the place evoked her Humboldt days. Scores of unwashed hippies, like her old roommate JJ, eating bottomless lentil soup at the old International Peasant. Thinking of JJ, she couldn't help but smile. She wondered whatever became of him.

The deserted reception desk and the roomful of unoccupied tables piqued Kit's curiosity. Was the restaurant even open today? Regardless, she ducked into the ladies' room to pee. Kit tamed her hair, applied lip gloss, then brushed a bit of powdered blush onto her cheeks. As she checked her reflection in the mirror, she questioned her outfit. She'd tried on a slew of tops, searching for a look that said casual, effortless attractiveness. Rejecting a half dozen or more, she remembered a top she'd gleaned from a Macy's clearance sale. For whatever reason, she'd never worn it. Now, as Kit smoothed the plush violet fabric of the velour pullover, she deemed it passable.

The outdoor terrace was a vision bathed in morning light. Waiters hovered, speaking in hushed tones as if in a sanctuary. Among the patrons seated at the perimeter, facing the sea, she spotted Joe. He wore a brown canvas jacket she'd never seen before, but she would have recognized that head of hair, that back, anywhere. Then, as if sensing her presence, he turned around, catching her. He rose from his seat, a huge grin lighting up his face. He hurried to her, playing out a scene in a romance movie.

Joe gave her a solid hug, a hug that felt like home. Inhaling the waxy-cottony scent of his jacket, the heady perfume of pheromones, the old familiar desire sparked.

So much for the home court.

Twenty-Five
San Francisco
March 30, 1981

Oblivious to Jonathan's gaze, Milo slurped his coffee. He shoveled eggs into his mouth, quickly swiped his lips with a napkin, then plunked his cup on the table. "Delicious," he proclaimed, rising from his chair. "Gotta go."

Jonathan's mouth set. He had been working too hard. "Already?"

He grabbed Jonathan's hands, yanking him to his feet. "Sorry, sweets," he said, giving him a big bear hug. "I have to stay with it. I promise, when this show is over, we'll live in bed for a week."

Jonathan breathed in the tang of his unwashed hair, both repellent and arousing. His hands gravitated from Milo's muscled shoulders to the small of his back, settling on his glorious ass. "But I miss you. Let's get back in bed right now," he murmured.

Milo gave him a chaste kiss. "I miss you, too," he said, backing away.

Jonathan dabbed a bit of jam from the corner of Milo's mouth. "Stay?"

"You know I can't."

Jonathan moaned. "Fine." His gaze dropped to Milo's stupendous erection, impossible to miss, even beneath baggy coveralls. It might have been comical if the fire had cooled. It had not. "Looks like your body has other ideas."

141

Milo grinned sheepishly. "Well, I can't do much about that." He grabbed his jacket and headed for the door.

Jonathan pictured him wearing his safety glasses, wrestling one of his outsize metal sculptures, sparks flying. "Why don't I come with you? Help you with the heavy lifting?"

In the end, Milo gently rebuffed him, as Jonathan had known he would, but at least he'd given it a shot. Milo's departure left him to sit with an unaccustomed feeling: loneliness.

Before Milo, he'd been solitary by nature, more or less fulfilled, content with the status quo. After all, he had Dylan, his greatest delight and challenge, at the center. Before Milo and Katherine resurfaced, drawn together by some unseen magnet, he'd felt nothing lacking. He hadn't realized a kind of stagnation had crept in; like an unseen virus, it had been deadening. A man needed disruption from time to time, lively discussions, opposing opinions. Change was good, as it turned out. The downside? He no longer liked being alone.

He settled in with his *Chronicle*, his second cup of Italian roast, hot and black as nature intended. He chuckled, recalling the way Milo heaped white sugar into his cup. On paper, they appeared unsuited, a glaring mismatch. Yet it worked, Milo the *yin* to Jonathan's *yang*, damn him. Unbathed and wearing paint-splattered coveralls, hair unkempt, he couldn't have been hotter.

Milo never failed to surprise him. His spontaneous, fun-loving, sex-hungry boyfriend had morphed. He hardly recognized the "new" Milo, the driven, preoccupied, hyper-focused artist. The new Milo left early, returned late, too exhausted for carnal activity. Instead of coming home to bed, he'd taken to napping on Kara's filthy cot. Jonathan respected his creative process and admired his talent. But he feared the old Milo might not come back. At any rate, he supposed he'd find out after the much-anticipated opening night.

Given Milo's recent surge in productivity and self-discipline, Jonathan felt comparatively inert. Oddly, he rather liked the feeling. He smiled, recalling the day he'd finally conceded defeat. After grappling at an impasse for untold hours, Jonathan acknowledged the agonizing truth. His novel had stalled—full stop. Unclenching his grip, his need to control, he'd simply let go.

The surrender loosened his mind, and the effect was immediate. No longer chained to his desk, released from his own tyranny, ideas had begun to percolate. Images came in bright flashes or tiny glimmers, at odd times, in unexpected places. Inspiration struck while making the bed, doing dishes, or sweeping the floor. Characters visited his dreams, whispering messages in his ear. And when he awoke, a shadow of their presence remained.

He should have known better. No amount of jaw-clenching determination had ever yielded results. Sitting at his desk, glaring at his typewriter had never worked. His best writing originated from a source he couldn't name. The mystery, the wellspring, could not be forced. Creativity could not be rushed or bullied into an arbitrary timeline.

Invigorated, liberated, he laced up his shoes and headed outside for a brisk walk. The morning was bright, shirtsleeves-warm and cloudless, for a change. He glanced up at the slate-blue sky as he crossed the street, stopping in front of Beth's vacant apartment. The rental sign had been removed; presumably another tenant was on the way. A new person to occupy her rooms, her air.

A wave of sadness washed over him. Beth had vanished without a trace. He supposed he'd expected a goodbye at the very least, but at the same time didn't begrudge her wordless escape. Nevertheless, he would miss her. Her presence had touched him. Their friendship, further evidence that first impressions are often wrong.

Jonathan had thought her bitter, a grump. And clearly, she'd reviled his very existence. He'd known her steely side, her frailty. He'd witnessed a brave, fierce mother trying to save her child. Squinting into her front window, he thought about the last night he'd seen her, when Jamie died. He thought about all the young kids who'd traveled to San Francisco in search of some mythic '60s flower power utopia, and there were thousands. Jamie had been only one of many gay boys who came here seeking refuge and ended up lost to the streets. Not a statistic, but someone's precious son, another soul whose ghost would forever haunt this city.

Jonathan had done it again. He'd shopped for the best ingredients and lovingly prepared another of Milo's favorite dishes. He should have known better, since the man couldn't be bothered with trivial things, like eating. Resigned to another solo dinner, Jonathan opened his book as he listlessly forked a bite of chicken.

The kitchen door bumped open, letting in a refreshing breath of air.

Jonathan glanced up to find Katherine, pretty in her faded jeans, peasant shirt, and strappy sandals, and couldn't help but grin. "Hey, stranger."

"Hey," she said, eyeing his bowl.

"Join me?" he asked.

"I thought you'd never ask."

He rose from his seat. "Allow me," he said, glad for her company. He ladled a generous portion of chicken and dumplings into her bowl and artfully sprinkled fresh parsley on top, then set the heaping bowl before her. "Voila."

Katherine's eyes widened. "Wow, this looks beautiful."

Jonathan had to agree. Tender chicken and veggies with homemade dumplings—the dish was gorgeous. "Thanks."

"What's the occasion?"

"No real occasion," Jonathan said. Zeke instantly appeared at his heels, purring and headbutting his ankles. He gently nudged the cat away. "Not for you, kitty."

"Well, it smells amazing," Katherine said. She slurped a big bite. "And it tastes even better."

For a petite woman, she could pack it away. He passed her a thick slice of warm sourdough bread along with the butter.

"Did you bake this?"

"I did. Actually, it's Milo's favorite."

"Unbelievable. You're so talented, you should have your own cooking show like Julia Child. Seriously, you could write a cookbook." She nodded knowingly. "Speaking of Milo, where is that boy?"

"Working." Jonathan frowned. "He's always working." Aware of his pouty tone, he added, "I realize he's focused on his show."

Katherine dabbed her lips with a napkin. "If it's any consolation, it's temporary. He used to disappear on me for days."

"Up in Humboldt?"

"Yeah, he's famous for it. Whenever he gets his head into a new sculpture, he obsesses, you know? And now, if you think about it, he's juggling multiple pieces and freaking out about the show." She took a breath. "When you factor everything in, it's quintessential Milo to the nth power."

Jonathan rubbed the stubble on his chin, unconvinced. "You're probably right."

"Don't worry," she said, meeting his gaze. "I promise you; he'll be back. He always comes back. He's loyal like a puppy."

Jonathan smiled. Katherine understood Milo in ways he never would, their shared confidences and mutual giggles a secret language he'd never speak. He'd only begun the journey, getting to know Milo's complexity, his quirks and eccentricities. Enjoying the ride, he counted himself lucky. "Thanks for the pep talk," he said. "But enough about me. How's your romantic life?"

She coughed out a laugh. "Nonexistent."

"Is that so?" he said, taken aback.

"Pretty much."

The little Jonathan knew of Katherine's personal life he'd gleaned secondhand, from Milo. She hadn't opened up to him lately and he didn't want to pry. "But what about Joe? I thought you two were back in touch."

Katherine recoiled slightly. "We were." She exhaled defeatedly. "It's over."

"I'm sorry."

"I suppose Milo told you we got together in Big Sur?"

He nodded. "I may have heard something along those lines."

Katherine gave him a skeptical look.

"Okay, he told me."

"It didn't turn out the way I thought it would," she said.

"How so?"

"We tried to recapture what we had, I suppose. But we're not the same people anymore. I'm not twenty-two." She shook her head. "It felt off, like we'd

145

outgrown each other. He'll always be my first love, but I'm not in love with him anymore."

Jonathan gave her a pointed look. "You can't force these things."

"Ah, now you tell me," she quipped. "It appears I've messed things up with Ben." Her face fell. "He got really angry when he found out I'd lied to him."

"Does that mean Ben is out of the picture?"

She raised an eyebrow. "Let's just say things have cooled."

"Is that what you want?"

Katherine shrugged. "Maybe I should swear off men altogether."

"Well, that is one option."

She pondered the idea, her smile returning. "No man at all—that sounds pretty good right now."

He studied her expression, aware of the fragility beneath her smile. "How about your writing?" he asked, sidestepping the touchy subject. "How's that going?"

She chuckled. "It's going pretty well. I've been experimenting," she hedged.

"What have you been working on?"

"Essays mostly. A young woman's take on politics, dating, that sort of thing." She glanced down. "I've actually submitted a few."

His fledgling had taken flight. "Excellent. Where?"

"You know, women's magazines, newspapers."

"That's a great strategy," he said, slightly wounded that she hadn't consulted him. "Keep me posted."

She smiled at him. "I will."

He met her eyes and forgot his bruised ego. If only he could impart some gem, some sparkling wisdom to guide and protect her, but what did he know? "How about dessert? I have chocolate chip ice cream."

She brightened. "Definitely."

Bowls of ice cream in hand, they ambled into the living room and sat together on the couch. Jonathan switched on the TV, hoping to catch the evening news.

The grim-faced news anchor reported, "Today President Reagan exited the Washington Hilton via *President's Walk*. Apparently on his way to his waiting limousine, a gunman fired six shots. The president was shot in the left lung, the bullet just missing his heart. He is currently at George Washington University Hospital and is listed to be in stable condition."

Jonathan stared at the TV in stunned silence. First Lennon. Now an attempted assassination of the president in broad daylight? Something had to be done about all the goddamn guns.

"Unreal," Katherine breathed. "The world has gone insane."

He gave her hand a squeeze. "That about sums it up."

ACT THREE

Twenty-Six
March 31, 1981

Kit jiggled open the tiny window above her desk, letting in a breath of spring. The mild afternoon called to her, tempting her away from her word processor. Stepping outside, she shed her sweatshirt and tied it around her waist. With no destination in mind, she ambled down the block and crossed over to Lincoln, into Golden Gate Park. She strolled past the conservatory and the botanical gardens, then stopped to admire the cherry trees in bloom. Kit appreciated the formal landscape, but she was drawn to the park's hidden unmanicured places.

She cut down a narrow meandering path, filling her lungs with woodsy scents. As she picked up her pace, she unleashed her cares, letting her mind travel without tether into the expanse of open space and possibility into the magic. Then she caught herself. Kit remembered the lessons taught. Like Little Red, alone in an isolated wood, she, too, must keep constant vigil. Ever alert, on the lookout for wolves lurking, her vulnerability the inescapable byproduct of gender. Just one goddamn time she'd like to mosey through the world without a care, the way men did. Maybe in the next life.

Kit circled back and was heading home when she noticed a weathered neo-classical building. Situated on the outskirts of the park, she'd likely passed it by many times without giving it a second thought. As she admired the stately building, she realized she'd stumbled upon a branch of the city library. With a faraway gaze, her thoughts drifting back to her school days.

While other students partied or goofed around, Kit inhabited the deserted nooks and hidden corners of the library. Books offered shelter, a refuge to recharge and collect her thoughts. Some of her earliest memories involved loving the library, and she knew exactly who to thank for that.

Her dad was an avid reader with an abiding respect for books. Kit recalled his preference for nonfiction, weighty tomes on politics religion and history. He'd visited their small, local library each week to replenish his pile, young Kit in tow. She'd wander the stacks and collect her own weekly ration. Back home, the two of them often read over dinner, side by side in companionable silence. By osmosis, she supposed, he'd inspired her love of the written word. Thinking of her father, a sudden sharp breath caught in her chest.

Kit yanked the open the glass door and stepped into the phone booth, shutting out the din from the street. She smelled the stale stench of urine, the black receiver, cool and weighty in her hand. "Hey dad," she said.

"Are you okay, honey?"

She heard the worry in his voice. "I'm great. I was out walking, and I was just thinking about you, Dad."

"Good thoughts, I hope."

"Of course."

"How's your schedule? Do you have time to meet your old dad for lunch this week?"

Kit chuckled. "I think that can be arranged," she said. Her gaze turned to a frowning, impatient-looking woman outside the booth, staring a hole through the glass. "Look, I'd better go. There's some lady outside glaring at me. I'll call you later."

Kit replaced the receiver and nodded to the woman as she made her exit. Then without hesitation, she strode up the library steps and entered through the ponderous door. Kit's romance with libraries ran deep, and this one did not disappoint. As she inhaled the musty air of reverential silence, it was like coming home. Kit approached the circulation desk, and to her delight, the bearded clerk bestowed her with a temporary card and the privileges therein.

She hit the nonfiction stacks first, removing and replacing volumes, touching, smelling, absorbing the tactile pleasure that for her, only books fulfilled. The choice was dizzying, but she settled on Studs Terkel's *Working*. She picked up a book on vegetarianism, then nabbed a do-it-yourself Volkswagen repair paperback with the intention of learning to change her own oil. Perhaps morbid curiosity drew her to *Helter Skelter*, an account of the infamous Manson murders, a book she'd deliberately avoided for years. Grizzly crime shit—*not* her thing.

Yet as she ran a hand over the smooth black jacket with its jagged-looking red script, something compelled her to open it. She glanced at the section of gruesome photos and with a shudder returned the book to the shelf. Kit left nonfiction and was browsing the fiction shelves when it struck her. Charlie Manson claimed that the Beatles spoke to him through their music, driving him to kill. The irony saddened her. John Lennon's advocacy for peace and non-violence, his voice forever gone. Against her better judgment, Kit went back for *Helter Skelter*, and the chilling saga kept her glued to the page until the wee hours.

The next day, Kit woke bleary-eyed and disoriented, the horrid book splayed open on her chest. The oily residue of fear still clung to her, leaving her remorseful, hungover, and queasy, like the time she scarfed a whole family-sized bag of Doritos in one sitting. What a waste of time and brain space. She'd managed to obliterate the better part of the past twenty-four hours absorbed in grim voyeurism. Kit sat up in bed, slammed the book shut and squinted at the calendar above her desk. April 1. How fitting. She laughed dryly. **The joke was on her.** And the worst part was, she'd done it to herself.

On her way to the bathroom, she peeled off her pajamas and tossed them onto the floor. She twisted the knob and stepped into the shower, savoring the delicious near-scalding water as it streamed over her head and down her body. She shampooed her hair with abundant lather, loofaed the dreadful Manson horror from her flesh, her soul. When she felt cleansed, Kit stepped out of the shower, her skin raw and red from the heat, and she took a hard look at herself in the mirror. She knew her reflection well. The thin nose with its spray of freckles. The wavy brown hair. The hazel eyes, not quite symmetrical.

On a whim she experimented with facial expressions, trying out her goofy face, her pretty face. She angled her chin, turned her head in search of her better side. As she pondered her "self," a disquieting thought occurred to her. Who was Katherine Hilliard, Kathy, Kit, Kit-Kat? Who was the girl—the woman— in the mirror? And what did it mean to be a woman?

With a towel snug around her body, she flopped back on the bed, her mind reeling. In New York, at least she'd had her own place, a job, and some semblance of a social life. But what did she have to show for her time in California? Had it been a mistake to move back? Her social life was practically nonexistent. In the past week she'd gone to Pacifica to celebrate her dad's fifty-ninth birthday. It had been wonderful to connect with him, the Crab Louie scrumptious, but a parent was no substitute for a peer. Did she have any peers?

In need of an ear, Kit ran down her options. The obvious choice—Joe. It would be so easy to pick up the phone and talking to Joe would ease her anxiety for the short term. But love was a slippery slope and Kit had to stay strong. Backsliding was not an option. She also couldn't call Ben. He'd made it clear he needed "time apart" to "sort things out." And Milo, her kindred, had vanished into his art, a private universe she couldn't begin to penetrate. How quickly she'd come to rely on her old pal's presence. Without him, she felt a little lost.

She thought about turning to Jonathan—again. But lately she'd suspected she'd worn her welcome thin. Between his novel and teaching, Jonathan's plate was full. Now that spring was here, the weather warmer, he probably wanted his studio back. His relationships with Milo and Dylan were primary; he'd found his triad. He didn't need a fourth wheel mucking up the works.

In a moment of clarity, Kit confronted the unvarnished, unavoidable truth. She needed to change, to expand her circle—she needed to get the fuck out of this studio—now.

She ponytailed her hair and dressed quickly, throwing on jeans, a t-shirt and sneakers. As she zipped her jacket, a wave of awareness washed over her. Countless times she'd worn the identical hairstyle and similar clothing without thinking. These were trivial things, she conceded. But what else in her life had become mechanical? What about the big important stuff, like captaining her own course? Shit. Had it been her choice to move to San Francisco? Had she ever truly chosen anything in her entire life?

As Kit shouldered the door open, the glassy tinkle of Milo's windchimes drew her gaze to the eaves. The chimes swayed, releasing their sweet music. Notes floated in the air like ripples in a stream, seeping into her, soothing her at her center. Out of the corner of her eye, she glimpsed Zeke, tigerlike, stalking through the overgrown grass. The cat bounded straight into the studio, then dashed back outside. "Crazy kitty," she said with a laugh.

Kit raised her face to the yellowy sun hanging in the vast translucent sky. She smelled the grassy air and smiled at the universe, no longer quite so daunting. As she exhaled, she let her worries go with the breeze. She picked her way down the pockmarked sidewalk to her faithful little bug, and as she gathered momentum, a conscious, deliberate plan took shape. The Ben situation must be settled today, regardless of consequences. He'd left her hanging too long and she couldn't abide the uncertainty, the dead air. How much time did a man need to figure out if he still wanted her? If he wanted to break up with her, so be it. It sure as hell beat limbo.

On a hunch, Kit drove to the station. She hit every green light and to her amazement landed parking only a block away, which she took as a positive omen. As she approached the garage, Kit recalled the first time she met Ben. She'd battled her way through airport traffic in that ill-fated rental, hopelessly lost. Exhausted, worried, and desperate to see her ailing father, she'd hit her breaking point. In keeping with what she now understood to be Ben's character, he'd come to her rescue.

Kit ducked into the garage, inhaling the dank, oily smell—off-putting, enticing. She spotted Ben in the office, his nose predictably in a book. "Hey, mister, I'm totally turned around. Can you help me find my way?"

Ben looked up, a stunned expression on his face.

Kit took a step back. "Hi," she croaked. Sorry to barge in on you."

He closed his book, resigned. "It's okay. Do you want to talk?"

Ben suggested they go to Eddy's, a favorite local dive. After Arlo agreed to cover for him, Kit followed him outside. Ben didn't take her hand as they strolled down the sidewalk in brittle silence. He didn't hold the door open for her upon their arrival.

"Where do you want to sit?" he asked.

Eddy's was between lunch and dinner shifts, so they had their choice of booths. "In back," Kit said.

Ben shrugged.

Kit studied Ben's face across the expanse of red Formica tabletop. He sipped his Coke, fiddled with his paper napkin, but did not speak. She finally broke the silence. "I wasn't honest with you about going to see Joe, and I'm really sorry. That was shitty of me." She grabbed his arm. "I promise, nothing happened. It's over for good."

He frowned. "I can't be with someone who isn't honest, Kit."

Kit's cherry soda burned the back of her throat. "I know."

Ben's face pinched in judgment. "You try?"

Her anger flared. How superior, how noble—how jerky he was. "Okay, Ben, I get it. I'm not like you. I've never volunteered for Peace Corps. I'm not heroic or selfless like you." Her gaze fell. "I'm not perfect."

He cringed. "I'm not looking for perfect."

"I just want to know where we stand." She groaned. "Are we broken up, or what?" It came out sounding whiny.

After a long moment, he reached across the table and squeezed her hand. "I hope not," he said.

She squeezed his hand back. "Me, too."

Ben leaned over the table to kiss her.

His lips were smooth and dry; his breath tasted of Coke. "Does this mean you're still coming to Milo's show with me?"

He got up, wedged in next to her, and kissed her again. "I wouldn't miss it."

April 12

Six days before Milo's show

"D-aa-d, it's starting," Dylan hollered. "Dad! It's about to launch!"

Jonathan folded the last of Milo's clean boxers with a sharp crease and positioned them neatly in his bureau drawer. "Coming!" he shouted. He finished tucking away his own clean socks and briefs. Although Jonathan didn't share Dylan's passion for all things NASA-related, he rushed to join him on the couch.

The television announcer enunciated each syllable, his tone fraught. When he began the final countdown, father and son chimed in. *Ten, nine, eight . . .*

A lot was riding on this, Jonathan thought. The nation still mourned the tragic accident that had killed two shuttle technicians, then bad weather had further postponed the mission.

"One!" Dylan squealed.

Liftoff occurred without a hitch—then, for a shaky moment, the craft disappeared behind a wall of white smoke. Along with the rest of the country, Jonathan watched and held his breath. When the shuttle broke through the billowing clouds, Jonathan's heart also soared. He imagined the astronauts hurtling into the unknown and choked up a little. Their journey held the promise of transcendence, hope for the future of humanity . . . or maybe he was just getting sappy in his old age.

"Extraordinary," Jonathan said.

"Extremely extraordinary," Dylan amended.

A little tap at the kitchen door dragged Jonathan back to earth. "That's the second time this week Katherine misplaced her key," he grumbled, but Dylan didn't seem to hear him. He got off the couch and made his way into the kitchen. But when he opened the door, Kara, not Katherine, waited on the stoop.

Kara cringed a little, her smile an apology. "I know, Jon. I'm early. I should have called."

Jonathan shook his head. "No, that's okay."

"I was hoping we could talk." She gave him a furtive look. "Privately."

"Don't worry. He's watching the space shuttle commentary. Completely engrossed."

Kara chuckled knowingly.

Jonathan liked their shared parental shorthand—when it came to Dylan, they spoke the same language. He held the door open for her. "Please, come in."

"Thanks," Kara said. She flumped down in the breakfast nook. "Whew," she said. "I'm beat."

"Wild night?" he kidded.

She snorted. "I wish."

"Can I offer you something to drink?"

"No. Well, maybe some pop if you have it."

Pop. He hadn't heard that expression since leaving the Midwest. Here, in California, they called it soda, or generically, coke. He rummaged through the fridge. "I have a Seven-Up," he said. "Will that do?"

"Perfect."

As Jonathan poured them each a glass, it dawned on him. Kara had always detested pop. Her sudden reversal left him uneasy for reasons he couldn't explain. "Is everything okay?"

Kara hesitated. She glanced up at the ceiling as if searching for the right response. "Yes, we're okay," she said.

Jonathan caught her fiddling with her ponytail, a sign of discomfort he knew well. "So, what did you want to talk about?"

She placed a palm on her stomach. "I'm pregnant, Jon."

He did a double take. How had he missed the high color in her cheeks, the weariness and the glow? He remembered how Kara's appearance had evolved when she'd carried Dylan. The weight gain and exhaustion, her belly growing like a melon, her transformation from mortal woman—to goddess. "That's great, right?"

"Yes," she said. "We weren't exactly planning on it."

"How far along are you?"

"Twelve weeks." Grief clouded Kara's face. "I guess I'm scared."

His throat went dry. "Scared?"

She nodded, resigned. "Well, I'm not exactly a spring chicken. I feel exhausted just thinking about the sleepless nights, the breast feeding—the diapers. And Kent is fifty-two. He'll be seventy when the little peanut graduates from high school."

Jonathan struggled for the right words to say. "Have you told Dylan?"

"No, but we're planning on telling him soon."

Jonathan envisioned the family portrait: Kent, Kara, Dylan and newborn baby gathered at the hearth. The tiny stab of jealousy in his gut turned to panic. "But you're staying in San Francisco, right?"

Kara appraised him skeptically. "Why wouldn't we?"

"I just assumed," he said with a frown. "You keep searching for a new gallery space. First Seattle, then Portland, then LA. I figured you might be thinking about moving."

"We've thought about it. But even if we do acquire something, we'll hire people to run it. We may need to travel more often, but we're not going to move, Jon."

His breathing leveled out. "I'm glad."

Kara continued. "Dylan loves his school. We wouldn't think of uprooting him."

Jonathan grinned at her. He treasured Kara. She loved Dylan unconditionally and with as much ferocity as he did. It seemed they'd come full circle. They were friends again, as they had been before marriage. Only this time around it felt real. "Kara?"

"Yes?"

"I'm really happy for you." He took a breath, let it out slowly. "You can count on me anytime you need a babysitter. If you ever need anything, I'm here."

Kara patted his hand. "I love you, too, Jon."

At that moment the air in the room changed. Jonathan sensed Dylan's presence. He glanced up and confirmed his hunch. "Hey, kiddo."

"Hey, you," Kara said.

"Hi, Mom. When did you get here?"

"A while ago. I got here a little early to talk with your dad. Are you ready to get going?"

Dylan shrugged. "I guess."

"Go and put your shoes on and grab your school stuff," Jonathan said. "And don't forget to check under the bed."

Dylan shuffled off and with the child out of earshot, Kara leaned in. "We're having a little get together before Milo's reception Saturday. Just a few art dealers, you know—drinks and hors d'oeuvres—that sort of thing. It's at our place. Around five thirty?"

"Sounds nice."

"Between us, it's really for Milo to meet some people informally, you know, before the public arrives."

"The public? Are you expecting a good-sized crowd?"

"I wouldn't be surprised, but you know how it is. You can never tell with openings." Kara paused for a breath. "Our guest of honor isn't exactly known for punctuality." Her lips formed a tight smile. "Can you make sure he arrives on time?"

Jonathan chuckled. "I will do my best."

That evening, as Jonathan put the kettle on for tea, he heard a distinctive clomp of footsteps on the back stairs. His heart jumped.

Milo lumbered in heavy-footed, but with a satisfied look on his face. "Hi lover."

"You're early," Jonathan remarked.

Milo slumped into Jonathan's waiting arms, heavy and limp like an overgrown, overtired kid. "It's done."

Jonathan kissed his cool, dry cheek. "Congratulations. How about a nice cup of tea?"

"Tea? Sorry, but that sounds unappealing right now."

"I can make you a snack, a plate of something," Jonathan offered.

"Thanks, sweetheart. But nothing. Really, I'm just so tired," Milo groaned.

"Well, I'm not surprised; you haven't slept for a week."

Milo grabbed a handful of Jonathan's shirt. He tugged him closer. "Any other suggestions, cowboy?"

Jonathan breathed heavily into his ear. "I'd say we'd better get you to bed."

April 14

Four days before Milo's show

A monster hankering for raw almond butter compelled Kit to return to Harvest. As she entered the shop, she was assaulted by the universal health food store smell, a pungent meld of yeasty powders and potions—revolting. She passed the community bulletin board with its confusion of ads when a poster tacked on top caught her eye. The handwritten text read: *Fearless Wimmin~~Midnight Readings in the Park.* The feminist twist on the spelling of "women" transported Kit to her college days and the women's studies classes she'd taken. She recalled how the classes had fired her up, influenced and informed her worldview. She tried to conjure the spirit of those times and that fiery girl she'd once been. But the feelings felt faraway, the girl barely visible behind a cloudy pane of glass.

"You dig poetry?"

Kit's heart jumped. After a quick glance around, she realized that the person at the cash register was talking to her. "Poetry? I guess. I mean, I like some of it," she said.

The cashier was a young woman about Kit's age. She busted out laughing. "Yeah, I know what you mean. A lot of it is pure shit drivel." Her expression sobered a bit. "But you should come. Check it out."

Tiny wings flitted in Kit's stomach. "I might."

"Far out. I'm Jesse, by the way."

Kit was drawn to Jesse's breezy vibe, long red kinky hair and faded denim painter's overalls. She stepped closer. "I'm Kit."

"Cool. Very wild west, like Kit Carson."

Kit's eyebrow arched. "Or Jesse James?"

"Touché."

A professional-looking dad wearing a baby backpack entered the store. He smiled at Kit as he approached the register. She bent down to peek at his little passenger, dozing contentedly, cheeks pink with sleep. The little guy was so adorable, Kit momentarily lost her train of thought. Like flipping a switch, she remembered Jesse and snapped out of it. "Are you a poet?"

Jesse let out a deep, rolling laugh. "Kind of."

Her uninhibited laughter put Kit at ease. She liked this girl. "So, I take it you're one of the fearless. When's your reading?"

"Tonight," Jesse said. She tilted her head, and scrutinized Kit as though reading her with a magnifying glass. "You write, don't you?"

A dry chuckle stuck in Kit's throat. "Kind of."

Jesse absently picked up an avocado sandwich rife with alfalfa sprouts. She took a lusty bite as mayo leaked down the heel of her hand to the counter. "Come read tonight, Kit Carson."

Thrilled and a little terrified at the prospect of hanging out with Jesse, as well as highly distracted by her leaky sandwich, Kit attempted nonchalance. "Maybe."

Jesse shrugged. "Well, if you want to come, meet me at The Wall. I'll be there around ten."

The man with the baby stepped up to the counter with a basket full of groceries. Kit moved aside for him then peeked again at the baby, awake now and drooling—so cute. An unfamiliar pang akin to hunger gnawed at her. Fuck. Did this mean she wanted a baby? She swallowed hard. "The wall?"

As Jesse began to ring up the man's groceries, she caught Kit's eye. "Yeah. You know, the club over on Haight."

Kit found herself nodding vigorously, as if she'd heard of the place. Then she left empty-handed, her craving for almond butter forgotten.

Kit sat cross-legged on the floor of the studio sorting her latest writing into two piles: *maybe* and *hell no*. Though the prospect of reading her work again in public had enlivened her, thus far, nothing stood out. She considered digging up one of her old pieces, but it felt like recycling—or worse, copping out.

The door wiggled and Milo shoved in. "Hey, Kit-Kat."

"Holy shit. Look what the wind blew in."

He sat down on the floor next to her, giving her a one-arm hug. "Yeah, I know. It's been a while."

Kit nestled into his embrace. "I've missed you so much."

"I've missed you, too, Kitty-Kat."

"How's your show going?"

Milo raised his arms like a Baptist preacher. "Halle-goddamn-lujah, it's done."

"Congrats."

"It's a huge relief," he said, reaching for one of Kit's papers. "What's all this?"

Kit snatched it from his hand. "Nothing, really. I'm just going through some of my new work. I'm thinking about going to this poetry thing tonight."

Milo let loose a grin. "How radical of you."

"Funny. Anyway, I met this girl—Jesse. She invited me." Kit scooped up all the papers and guarded them in her lap. "It's been several eternities since I've read in public. I can't decide if I even want to do it." She huffed. "Shit, I don't think I'll go."

Milo's expression told Kit he saw through her. "Life is fleeting, my dear. Throw your hat in the ring while you can."

Kit couldn't argue with that wisdom nugget. "Come with me?"

He shrugged. "What time?"

"It starts at midnight."

Milo coughed out a laugh. "Midnight?" He paused, letting it sink in. "I would, but Jon and I are going on a day trip tomorrow. You know how he is." He rolled his eyes. "He'll want to leave at dawn. What about Ben? Can't he go with you?"

Kit's face scrunched. "I doubt he'd be interested."

Milo squeezed her shoulder. "Are you guys okay?"

"It's confusing. We're not, *not* together, but we're not really together, you know?"

His brow furrowed. "That's confusing. Is it what you want?"

Kit's stomach bottomed out. Did she want to be with Ben? She gave Milo a playful shove. "I wish you were coming," she said, regretting her whiny tone.

"I promise I'll come to the next one, okay? And don't worry. You're gonna kill it."

She dropped the stack of papers back on the floor. "Oh yeah? What makes you so sure?"

"You're Katherine Hilliard," he said matter-of-factly. With that, he kissed her cheek and then rose shakily to his feet. "See you later, sweets."

Kit gazed up at her friend as he towered over her. She sensed something vaguely wrong but had no words to explain her perception. "Hey, Mi, are you alright? You look a little worn out."

He shook his head. "No, I'm fine. I just woke up, that's all."

She checked the clock on her nightstand. Four thirty in the afternoon— late, even for Milo, the king of sleeping in. A tiny shudder passed through her, so subtle she dismissed it.

Milo turned to leave, then hesitated at the threshold. "Knock 'em dead, Kit-Kat." He flashed her a grin then slipped out.

Kit laughed. Quintessential Milo. On the verge of his first major art show, an event fraught with meaning and genuine consequence, he had to be freaking out. Yet he found the grace to comfort her about a piddly, insignificant reading. With flinty resolve Kit got up off the floor. She grabbed a notebook and pen, then let the ink spill onto the page.

Invisible Man

Stalker, Rapist, Charlie Manson
I see you

You follow me
Wherever I go
In my head or in the flesh
The threat

A low hum, a whisper, a sneer, a fist

I see you, invisible man
And still, I step into the night
I wear what I want, think what I want, go where I want—do what I want.
I want
I own my body, my life

And I will not be afraid

Kit read her scrawl aloud. Not great—not terrible—it would do. She figured tonight's audience would be forgiving, her reading low stakes, a chance to dip her toe into the shallow end. Still, the very thought of exposing her work to the public sparked the old jitters. Even now, she vividly recalled the cold sweats and the times she'd ducked into the bathroom to vomit before a bookstore appearance. Yet when she took the stage, Katherine Hilliard took over.

Kit set the poem aside and powered up her word processor. She scrolled down the screen to revisit one of her recent pieces, a young woman's take on San Francisco's shifting culture. In the moment she'd finished it, deep in her bones, she'd known—it was good. Before she could second guess it, she'd printed it out, sealed it in an envelope and dropped it in the mailbox.

Hell, yes. She was Katherine Hilliard.

At 10:45 p.m., Kit stood on the cracked sidewalk to confront The Wall. She'd envisioned a pulsating nightclub or dive bar, not the bland storefront before her eyes. Indeed, she would have missed it entirely, thinking it a generic shoe repair shop or dry cleaners, if she hadn't driven around the block three times with eyes peeled. Her doubt mushroomed but she shoved through the door anyway.

The place was packed, the faint odor of pot in the air. People were clustered at small, jumbled tables while others stood huddled in conversation. Kit hung back by the door, taking in the sea of ironic army jackets, denim, and halter tops. As she searched for Jesse's red mane, her gaze traveled the length of one red brick wall to its anchor, the bar, teeming with patrons. There Kit spotted Jesse—she hoped—at the far end. She struggled out of her coat, sweating through her deodorant, then elbowed and threaded her way to the bar.

Jesse sprang up from a barstool, waving her hands like a traffic cop. Kit waved back. Jesse yelled something but Kit couldn't make out a single word over the clash of conversation and background music. She kept moving forward, determined to reach Jesse. "Jesse James," she cried.

She charged Kit, wrapping her in a crushing hug. "Kit Carson! You made it."

Kit took in her flowy caftan, black jeans, and knee-high boots. The art of fashion eluded Kit, and Jesse's chic, effortless style impressed her. "You look fantastic."

Jesse beamed at her. "Thanks." She considered Kit for a moment. "You look great, too."

Kit rolled her eyes. "Well, at least I changed out of my sweatshirt."

Jesse mimicked her with an exaggerated eye roll.

Kit studied her as she nonchalantly twisted a hank of hair and knotted it into a bun on top of her head, where it remained magically in place. This woman was a sorceress. In her presence, Kit felt giddy, yet a little paranoid of falling under her spell.

"Jesus, it's hot in here. Want a beer?" Jesse asked. With a wave she summoned the bartender, then returned to Kit. "Beer?"

Kit wasn't eager for the foamy brew. These days, she preferred wine. "Sure," she said, vaguely aware of her need to impress this woman, a virtual stranger. She'd sensed a rare kinship with Jesse and didn't want to blow it. On the periphery, she noticed two guys orbiting. "Do you know those guys?"

Jesse acknowledged them with a nod, and the guys shuffled over. "Kit, these two freaks are Noah and Mason. She draped a lazy arm around Kit. "And this is Kit—she's a writer."

"Cool," the taller guy said.

Heat coursed through Kit's body. Was this a setup? A blind date? If so, which boy was hers? Before she had a chance to decide, an earsplitting crash turned her head. Amid the clamor and commotion, Kit zeroed in on the cocktail waitress. The poor woman had dropped her tray and was on her knees picking up broken glass. Kit knew plight, all too well. She recalled one particularly grim experience from her Waffle Hamlet days—on her hands and knees, stoically collecting shattered glass while tables full of drunken customers barely contained their guffaws. Without hesitation, she stormed up, reached out a hand and helped the waitress to her feet.

By the time she returned to the bar, Jesse and the guys had vanished. Her heart plummeted, her mind jumping to the worst case—she'd been ditched. She'd been wrong about Jesse. They were not destined to be friends. Kit gulped the unpleasant beer then ordered another—when in Rome. She drained it then drifted away from the bar.

Kit was making her exit when a pair of hands grabbed her shoulders. "Are you leaving?"

She twisted around to confront Jesse. "No," she lied.

Jesse gave her a dubious frown.

Kit avoided her eyes. Her shoulder twitched involuntarily. "I don't know, I guess I thought you ditched me."

"What the hell? I thought *you* ditched *me*."

Kit hacked out a chuckle. Maybe her intuition had been right about Jesse after all. A warm wave of relief washed over her. "Where'd you go, anyway?"

"Bathroom," Jesse said with a grimace. "I got my period." She wrinkled her nose in disgust then leaned in closer. "Had to make do with a wad of toilet paper."

Kit nodded knowingly in solidarity with Jesse and every woman on the planet. "That's the worst."

"Yeah. And when I finally came out of the bathroom, this dude cornered me and wouldn't shut up. I looked for you at the bar."

Kit fished around in her bag but came up empty-handed. "Sorry, I usually have a tampon on me."

Jesse shook her head. "That's okay. I'm good." She opened her palm to display a tiny red glass pipe. "Hey, do you want to get high?"

After undergrad, Kit had pretty much sworn pot off. "Hmm."

Jesse grinned as she threw the door open. "Let's get the hell out of here."

Kit trailed behind Jesse as she turned the corner and stopped at the entrance of a dark alley. Her rational mind kicked in, churning out questions. Holy shit. Was she that far gone? Would she follow this dangerous girl anywhere?

Rapt, Kit kept her eye on Jesse's practiced hand as she sparked her cute little pipe. Jesse took a long hit, her face momentarily aglow in the light of the flame, then passed it to Kit.

Kit didn't second-guess it. She inhaled the harsh smoke deep into her lungs, then coughed it out. After another toke or two, they set out for the park. Kit buttoned her coat against the chill, taking in the city, unrecognizable now, enfolded by the night. Beneath a starless black sky, the urban heartbeat drummed in Kit's ears, in sync with her footfalls. And with Jesse by her side, the very air crackled with possibility.

April 15
Three Days Before Milo's Show

As Jonathan merged northbound onto the Golden Gate Bridge, he turned to glimpse the shadowy silhouette of the worker marooned inside Beth's tollbooth. Memories of his former neighbor, a former toll taker—former mom—rushed in. He wondered briefly if she'd found solace with her family in Arizona. Jonathan pictured her on her stoop smoking a cigarette, her small body diminished by grief. A painful snatch of breath caught in his throat like a warning. If he didn't entertain such thoughts, he would be protected from unspeakable, unfathomable loss. Or so he told himself.

The sky abruptly cracked open, dumping buckets of rain onto the windshield. Blinded by the deluge, Jonathan flipped on the wipers, which were useless. "I can't see a damn thing," he muttered.

Milo stirred. "Fine day for a road trip."

Jonathan's shoulders calcified. "Quit griping."

Milo let out an enormous, oblivious yawn. "Well, it is eight in the morning."

Jonathan didn't make a habit of snapping at those he loved, but lately Milo had worn his patience thin. He stole a glance at his erstwhile vivacious sweetheart, slumped like a ragdoll. Although Milo had gone to bed early last night, he'd woken up groggy. In fact, the man had slept through most of the past two days. Milo couldn't be bothered to pick up his socks, make the bed, or wash a dish. And in his state of exhaustion, his company hadn't been exactly scintillating.

Jonathan was so wrapped up in his list of gripes, he didn't notice the clouds as they drifted, then parted like a curtain. The gloom yielded to reveal a bright blue sky as the last few droplets flurried and scattered on the windshield. Jonathan clicked off the wipers and turned his gaze to the sun. He exhaled, and the tightness in his shoulders released. He glanced over at Milo snoring adorably and felt his heart soften. Poor guy. The stress of his show had really taken a toll on him.

As if he could read Jonathan's thoughts, Milo perked up.

"I thought you were out cold," Jonathan said. "Welcome back."

"Hey, where'd the rain go?"

Jonathan shook his head. "I know. Damn crazy California weather."

"I love it," Milo breathed.

Jonathan massaged Milo's shoulder, his left hand steady on the steering wheel. "Rest if you want, hon. I'll wake you when we get to the Russian River."

"Nah, I'm awake now," Milo said. "I don't want to miss this. The air's so sparkling clear. It's . . ." He hesitated, searching for the right word. "Dazzling," he concluded.

The surface of the bay shimmered. With the air washed clean, sunlight scattered like glitter on the wet pavement. Jonathan lifted his gaze to the bridge's dusky orange pillars framed by blue sky then turned to Milo, overcome with the fullness of his life. "You're the dazzling one," he said.

"I love you, too, Jon. Sorry I've been such a pain."

"Not a pain. Just a mild irritant."

Milo unleashed one of his megawatt grins. "Well, I *could* make it up to you," he said coyly as his fingers tiptoed up Jonathan's thigh.

Jonathan snatched Milo's hand, holding on for dear life as his tires careened into the next lane. He righted the car. "Whoa, let's not get ourselves killed right before your show."

Milo interlaced his fingers with Jonathan's. "I suppose you're right. I'm just saying, it's been a while."

"We *could* pull over," Jonathan said suggestively.

Milo jerked his hand away. "Damn, look at that," he said, wheeling around in his seat to gawk and point.

Jonathan, thrown off-kilter, figured there must have been a bad accident or maybe aliens had landed on the bridge.

"Over there," Milo continued. He pointed to the craggy hillside, flushed purple with wildflowers. "The larkspur—they're blooming like crazy."

Catching a glimpse of the vibrant landscape, Jonathan impulsively veered off the highway. He drove into the Marin Headlands, nosed the Volvo into a parking spot on the shoulder, and cut the engine. His hand clapped Milo's knee. "Are you up for a walk?"

"Definitely," Milo said, already popping the car door open.

They set out on a narrow dirt path that meandered up the hillside. Milo, with his long limbs, climbed like a mountain goat. Jonathan slogged behind, winded and mildly annoyed, but when he reached the crest, his efforts were rewarded. Jonathan took Milo's hand, and for a long while they stood in silence. He gazed at the bridge's graceful cables, the city beyond its gates. He looked down at the parade of tiny cars moving on the bridge and it struck him. Moments ago, they'd been right there—in one of those tiny cars.

Jonathan met Milo's eyes. "Quite a picture, wouldn't you say?"

Milo put an arm around him, pulling him close. "Dazzling."

Hand in hand, they departed from the trail and wandered into a field dense with wildflowers. They bushwhacked, their feet crunching the wild grasses that released sweet herbal scents into the air. Surrounded by tall waving grasses, they shed their clothing and made a bed of jackets and earth. And as they lay together, bodies intertwined, the larkspur bowed their purple heads and watched over them.

They'd arrived home around eight that evening. Milo, dead tired, had kissed Jonathan goodnight and gone straight to bed. Left to his own devices, Jonathan considered the work he'd been neglecting. Instead of marching straight to his office like a good soldier, he arranged three chocolate chip oatmeal cookies on a pale blue Fiesta plate. He made a pot of peppermint tea, carried his snack into the living room, and flopped down in his reading chair. It had been quite a long day, and in that moment, he wanted nothing more than to sit quietly with his thoughts.

He experienced a low-grade uneasiness as he sipped his tea but didn't understand why. Overall, the trip to Guerneville had been enjoyable. He'd heard many tales—mostly from Milo—of the legendary gay retreat on the Russian River. But he'd been unprepared for the multitude. Other than in the Castro, he'd never seen so many boys. Legions of boys. Flocks of boys, holding hands on the street. All kinds of boys—old and young, muscled and shirtless—bears.

Going to Guerneville had been Milo's idea. He'd wanted Jonathan to get a taste of the scene, hoping to convince him to return for a longer stay. Milo had spent a lot of time there, sewing oats in the late seventies, while Jonathan had lived a very different, relatively solitary life with Dylan.

He didn't begrudge Milo's history, wasn't jealous of his many sexual escapades—or maybe he was, a little. In truth, he'd felt ill at ease amid the throng at Fife's resort. Milo had been in his element, but Jonathan felt out of his depth. Still, he'd promised Milo they'd come again soon for a few days of R&R. Jonathan finished off a cookie, licking a smudge of chocolate from his fingertips. Yes, he had serious reservations about Guerneville. But Milo was worth the effort.

With a faraway smile, he replayed the details of their sublime morning. First, the drenching rainstorm that vanished as quickly as it had appeared, then their impromptu interlude in the hills of Marin. He couldn't help but grin as he recalled—and there was no polite way to put it—their heated, urgent fuck. But it had been more than that. What happened in that field of flowers hadn't been solely physical. Jonathan experienced a pure loving energy pulsing through them, a sensation that eclipsed the earthly with the bodily. He'd felt transported, as if on a separate plane.

Of course, they eventually came back to earth. Milo had been cold, and Jonathan's leg felt itchy. As he brushed the dirt from his ass and collected his underwear, he'd glanced over at Milo fumbling with the buttons of his shirt. In that moment, like Suess's Grinch, Jonathan's heart expanded. As he buttoned Milo's shirt for him, he'd felt their bond deepen.

Jonathan was mildly startled when he realized he'd eaten all the cookies. He'd finished the tea. He set his cup on the end table to scratch at the angry rash on his thigh. With a faraway gaze, he smiled. *Damn Larkspur.*

April 17

One Day Before Milo's Show

The blaring phone yanked Kit from a pleasant dream into the stark light of day. She rubbed her eyes, stretched out a lazy arm, and picked up. "Hello," she said, her voice gravely with sleep. She overheard faint echoes, clinking sounds, perhaps paper rustling. "Hello?" she said again, but the caller seemed to have set the phone down. With a pang in her chest, she envisioned Ben hunched over medical charts. "Ben? Is that you?"

"Is this Katherine Hilliard?"

Kit drew a sharp breath. Not Ben. The unknown male voice rang authoritarian, older. She pushed and wriggled her way to a seated position. "Yes."

"Walt Travis," he said. "Features editor at the *Chronicle*."

Chilly pins pricked the skin of her forearms. Was she still dreaming?

"Let me cut to the chase," he said. "I've gone over your freelance piece." He paused. "It prints Sunday. That is, if it makes the final cut."

Kit pulled at the folds of her phone ear, oddly hot and itchy. Had she heard him correctly? "Sunday?"

He breathed heavily. "I can offer you forty bucks."

"Forty?" she asked dumbly.

"That's the going rate," he replied, his tone brusque.

Kit struggled to wrap her mind around it. When she'd dropped her submission into the mailbox, it had been her first go, for shit's sake. She'd expected zero for her efforts, not an acceptance.

He continued. "Look kid, I know the pay is shit, but it's a start. Katherine? May I call you Katherine?"

Kit finally grasped what the man was saying. "Yes. No! Forty's fine," she blurted. "Thank you."

He chuckled. "Listen, your writing needs polish, but it has potential. My advice would be to keep freelancing, build your chops. Between you, me, and the wallpaper, there's buzz at the paper for a byline to pull in the youth demographic. Keep working the, you know, *woman* angle."

Kit pictured him as the archetypal hard-boiled reporter—disheveled smoker, flask hidden in his cluttered desk drawer. His condescension subtly irritated her, but what the hell did she care if the guy was a chauvinist? Because *this* was happening—this was real. "Thanks for the advice, Mr. Travis," she gushed, playing up the fawning female.

"Call me Walt. And next time send your work to me directly," he said, then abruptly rang off.

Kit replaced the receiver and flew out of bed, her head spinning—in a good way. She snatched the folded newspaper, zeroed in on the ad circled in red. *One-bedroom sublet-Telegraph Hill.* Talk about luck. The place was cute, cheap and, incredibly, soon to be hers. And now, an actual editor from the *Chronicle* had just called her. Overcome with good fortune on this beautiful morning, Kit danced around the tiny studio, belting out her favorite *Oklahoma* ballad at the top of her lungs.

Kit eventually cooled down, parked herself at her desk, and got busy on a new freelance piece. Still abuzz from her spate of fortune, her words came fluidly, brain ignited, fingers fast. As she wrote, visions of her future took shape. She pictured herself plugging away in her little Telegraph apartment, Katherine Hilliard: columnist. She imagined Jesse, Milo, and Jonathan squished into her little kitchen, the images sharp in her mind. But when she tried to fit Ben into the picture, her clarity lessened.

In a mind-boggling few days, everything had changed. Kit credited Jesse, new friend and catalyst, for loosening the fabric of the universe. Their venture into Golden Gate Park at midnight was a mind-blowing rush. In that extraordinary place and time, Kit had felt part of something radical and consequential, an underground movement.

The turnout had been larger than expected, maybe fifty or sixty people huddled together on the lawn, faces illuminated by the soft glow of candlelight. Kit wedged in next to Jesse, hugging her knees to her chest. As she'd listened to each poet in turn, she absorbed every word, her mind literally expanding, or maybe it had just been the weed. Her own turn onstage marked the end of her dry spell and left her feeling both relieved and energized.

Kit's phone rang for the second time today, cutting through her daydream. "Hello," she breathed.

"Ma'am, this is Agent Parsons, FBI. I'm looking for a beautiful female body to investigate. I have reason to believe you fit the description."

Ben's "Sergeant Friday" impression was dead on. FBI—Female Body Inspector. Kit hadn't heard that one since sixth grade. She snorted. "Hardly."

Ben reverted to his usual voice. "Hey, I miss you. I'm starting to forget that gorgeous smile of yours."

Kit's neck prickled with heat. Ben had broken their last date. He'd been the unavailable one, but for unknown reasons she felt guilty. "I miss you, too," she fibbed.

"At least we'll see each other tomorrow."

Tomorrow? Kit had been so caught up in her own head lately, she'd completely forgotten about Milo's show—holy shit—tomorrow night. "Can't wait to see you. What time are you picking me up?"

"I just found out I have to work until six," Ben said, his tone weary.

Kit's heart sank. "But I thought you were off all day tomorrow," she said, unable to mask her disappointment.

"I thought so, too. I couldn't get out of it, Kit. We're shorthanded, especially in the ER. I'm really sorry."

Kit supposed Ben could hardly refuse a request from a supervising doctor. She acknowledged sleep deprivation as a key element of an intern's job description. Ben's brutal back-to-back shifts often left him distracted and bone tired. At times, Kit felt like one more chore on Ben's checklist, an added stressor on top of his demanding workload. He kept reassuring her that things would ease up soon. The last thing she wanted was to come off as a complaining girlfriend. "Don't worry, it's fine. I'll meet you at the gallery."

"I'll make it up to you. Take you to dinner after."

"Sounds great."

"Then, after dinner," he said as he unleashed an evil, lecherous laugh. "I'll take you to my bed."

"Oh, you will, will you?" Kit said. To keep up the flirty banter, she added, "Only if you wear your stethoscope and nothing else." She waited for Ben's comeback, but instead she heard him struggle to suppress a yawn.

Ben cleared his throat. "Sorry, I'd better grab a few hours of sleep."

"Okay, I'll let you go," Kit said. In that moment, melancholy washed over her.

When Kit returned to her writing, she found the trail had gone cold, her train of thought off the rails. With a groan, she gave up for the day. Kit shut off her word processor, and as she idly gathered her hair into a ponytail, her stomach complained. She'd been munching trail mix from the health food store all morning, but it left her feeling empty, gassy, and hungry for real food. She envisioned Jonathan stirring a steamy pot on the stove as tempting, delicious scents wafted in the air.

She hoofed up the back steps into the kitchen as starved for company as she was for a home-cooked dinner. To her dismay, no ambrosial aromas hung in the air—no Jonathan. With a sigh, she tugged the fridge open and lingered awhile, staring blankly at its contents.

"Find anything good?"

A shiver crawled up Kit's spine. She whipped around to find Milo at her heels. "Shit, you scared the hell out of me. You shouldn't sneak up on people."

Milo's eyebrow arched. "Guilty conscience, Kitty-Kat?"

Kit released the handle and the door whooshed shut. She frowned. "Look who's talking."

"Touché, ma chère," he said. He looked at her intently. "You okay?"

"Yeah. Except that I'm starving."

Milo chuckled, then enfolded her in his arms. "Well, that would explain your mood, miss grumpy pants."

Kit rested her head on his chest. "Sorry, Mi. I guess I am a little grumpy."

Milo patted her back. "All is forgiven."

Kit opened the fridge again. She foraged a brick of jack cheese she'd bought a week ago, broke off a hunk and popped it in her mouth. "Is Jonathan here?"

"It's not polite to talk with a mouthful of cheese, missy," he scolded. "Jon's in his office. He's been at it all afternoon."

"That's good, right?" Kit shrugged. "Well, I guess it's up to us."

"What's up to us?"

She held the fridge door open and peered inside. "We'll have to cook dinner."

Milo gave her a playful shove. "Fear not, my friend."

Kit shoved him back. "What do you mean?"

"Jon made a spinach lasagna this morning."

Kit's insides gurgled at the mere suggestion. "Ah, this must be it!" She unearthed a large glass casserole dish and set it down on the countertop. As she pulled back the foil to peek inside, the divine scent of marinara bright with garlic and rosemary traveled from her sinuses straight to the pit of her stomach. She gave Milo a hard look. "You, my friend, are one lucky man."

He met her gaze. "Don't I know it, sister."

They went to work with an easy, natural rhythm. While Kit preheated the oven and set the table, Milo assembled ingredients. In short order, salad and garlic bread had been readied, lasagna safely tucked into the oven. Kit was reminded of their days at Waffle Hamlet and smiled at their accomplishment. "We always were an efficient team."

"We were unbeatable," Milo said as he reached into the pantry. He extracted a bottle and with a grin held it aloft and wagged it at her. "Look what I found."

The sight of a vodka bottle struck Kit as incongruous, since Jonathan wasn't much of a drinker. "Maybe he's saving it for a special occasion," she suggested.

"No, I'm sure it's for me—us," Milo said. He unscrewed the cap, poured them each a shot, and joined Kit at the table. "Look at us, Kit-Kat. How did we end up here?"

"I have no idea whatsoever, but it's kind of nice, isn't it?"

Milo polished off his shot in one glug and poured himself another. "So, how was your midnight reading?"

In the fading light, Kit thought his face looked a bit drawn, but she didn't mention it. "In a word, trippy."

Milo leaned forward, his elbows on the table, chin cradled adorably in his palms. "Spill."

"You know, très beatnik, candles, and poetry."

"Sounds groovy. And you killed, right?"

Kit's reading in public had felt monumental at the time, but now it seemed a bit trivial. "I did okay."

Milo stared a hole through her. "What are you not saying, Kit-Kat?"

Kit picked up her shot glass, then took a small sip. "It's been a wild few days," she said. Unsure where to begin, she inhaled deeply, exhaled slowly. "I have some pretty big news. This morning an editor from the *Chronicle* called me out of the blue. They're going to publish one of my pieces."

Milo slammed his glass down on the table. "That's fucking fantastic." He grabbed her by the arm. "I'm so proud of you." He wore a faraway smile. "I've always known you'd make it big. This is just the beginning for you."

Kit flushed, then quickly dodged the compliment. "What about your accomplishments, mister? Look at you, on the eve of a major show. If anyone's proud, it's me."

"Thanks, sweets." His expression sobered. "I'm glad you're here with me."

As Kit looked into his beautiful brown puppy dog eyes, for reasons she didn't fully understand, she choked up. "I'm glad I'm here, too."

The air changed when Jonathan entered the kitchen. "Hey folks," he said. "Looks like you two have been busy."

Milo's face brightened. The light shifted away from Kit as he beamed at Jonathan. "Come join us, handsome. Lasagna's in the oven."

Later that night, Kit lay awake in bed, her mood contemplative. She remembered the moment she'd stepped off the plane and planted her feet on California ground—less than five months ago. She realized that the daily minutia of her former existence had begun to recede; New York had faded into broad strokes. Yes, there'd been the daily drudgery of commuting, the aching feet trapped in heels. Countless hours of ennui at Powell-Standish, lonely nights in her apartment. But she could no longer recall her inner life, emotions, and hopes. Somehow Kit's present had become her past.

Unbidden, her former officemate, the slow-witted Bradley, popped into her head. Unlike so many details, his smirk remained stubbornly lodged in her brain. No doubt he'd been promoted by now, like all the rest of his ilk, that is, with protruding genitalia. The old bitterness and resentment rose from her gut and clotted in her throat.

Kit had followed every rule, heeded every convention. Studied hard, worked hard, trusted in the system. She'd kept her head down, stayed the course, outshining the men. Still, opportunity eluded her. Her day never came. If news of her father's fragile heart hadn't called her home, she would still be there. The thing was, Kit hadn't realized her own heart had been unwell. Jonathan had seen her when she herself could not. She hadn't known she was drowning until he offered her a life preserver.

Tonight's dinner with Jonathan and Milo had been bittersweet. She'd waited for the right moment to break the news that she'd soon be moving out, but somehow it never felt right. And the longer she held back, the bigger it felt, heightening her awareness of the here and now. She'd taken for granted the lively banter and inside jokes, come to rely upon the comforts of familial friendship. The time had come to rely on herself, and like New York—like everything else on earth—this was fleeting. This place, this stage of life, would never be again. Kit would miss the way the sun slanted through her window in the early morning. She'd miss bright, inquisitive Dylan, his Legos and violin. The furry blur of Zeke chasing butterflies across the lawn. The taste of Jonathan's coffee, his restless mind and advice. Milo's goofy grin, his bullshit—his insistence on loving her.

April 18, 1981
The Morning of Milo's Show

At daybreak Jonathan rolled away from the light streaming in through the window. His sole desire on this day of days was to linger all morning in bed, to cuddle, have sex, and drift weightlessly back to sleep. To wake up and drowsily begin again—rinse—repeat. He sensed a slight tickle on his left shoulder blade, quite a delicate gesture for Milo. Aroused, he turned to open his arms to his man, but instead came face-to-furry-face with Zeke. The cat tunneled into Jonathan's chest, started up his purr-motor and, with grim determination, kneaded his paws.

"Jesus," Jonathan muttered as he tried to detach the cat's tiny stubborn claws, like fishhooks, stuck in his flesh. He yanked Zeke off like a Band-Aid, clutched him by his scruff, then unceremoniously released him to the rug. The cat landed on all fours with a muffled thud.

Jonathan scowled at his black silk pajama top, now riddled with claw pricks. He glanced over at Milo, snoring steadily, and envied him a little. The man could sleep through anything: thunderclaps, earthquakes, sirens. Jonathan knew better than to disturb him—never poke a hibernating bear. And today, on this day of days, he wanted everything to go smoothly for Milo. He crept out of bed, collected his robe and slippers, then slipped out of the room.

As Milo slept soundly, Jonathan made his way down the hallway to Dylan's door. Unable to resist, he turned the knob in practiced, soundless increments. He slightly cracked the door open like he'd done a thousand times. The boy lay child-splayed out on his back, a posture so vulnerable it brought a sudden hot tear to Jonathan's eye. For a long moment he tracked the rise and fall of his child's chest. Then, with a sweet ache in his heart, he quietly closed the door.

The weather gods had gone above and beyond, summoning a bright spring day for Milo's show. A fine day indeed, Jonathan mused, as he stepped outside to greet the day with a deep inhale of jasmine-scented air. He glanced up at the cloudless sky. When he bent to pick up the newspaper, Zeke materialized. The cat tentatively brushed up against his ankles, perhaps offering an apology for shredding his pajamas. He'd never been fond of felines and wasn't thrilled about playing surrogate parent. Nevertheless, the wayward tabby had claimed him. "If nothing else, I have to give you points for persistence," he told Zeke, and with a sigh, bundled the little fellow into his arms.

He headed into the parlor juggling cat and newspaper, then flumped gracelessly into his reading chair. A glance at his watch reminded him that Dylan would be up within the hour, groggy and wanting breakfast. And when Milo finally yawned into the kitchen, he'd want...what? No telling. Milo might be anxious or fragile, in need of propping up. Or maybe he'd be lighthearted and relaxed before his show. In reality, when it came to Milo's mood, Jonathan often had no idea what to expect. Today, he was prepared for anything and grateful for this solitary interlude before "show day" would begin in earnest.

He opened his paper, browsed the headlines, and turned to an article about a twin-engine commuter aircraft. The pilot collided head-on into a small private plane, killing fifteen. Jonathan was reminded of death's unpredictability, the fleeting nature of his own existence. Next, he read about a deadly coal mine accident that had taken fifteen lives as well. Disquieted, he set the paper aside. In that moment, Zeke wedged between the arm of the chair and Jonathan's rib cage and wriggled into his lap. Jonathan scratched the cat's head, absorbing the comfort of his warm little body and vibrating purr. He returned to his paper, thumbed through to the Arts and Entertainment section and zeroed in on the ad for Milo's show. Kara must have shelled out a small fortune. It filled several columns and stood apart from run-of-the-mill listings.

Envision Gallery Presents

Outside

Dimensional Creations

by Milo Archer

Artist's Reception 7:00 p.m.

The ad hit Jonathan with a reality gut punch. Sure, he'd known this day would come. But somehow, he'd pictured it in some remote and unseeable future—funny how the mind plays tricks. Would tonight be a triumph for Milo, one of many to come? Or would it be a disappointment—or worse, a setback?

So much was riding on it, Jonathan realized, that for weeks he'd been figuratively holding his breath. Like many creatives, Milo had never been grounded in the kind of day-to-day practicalities required to achieve commercial success. Although he'd never doubted Milo's genius, he feared people simply wouldn't "get" it. Milo's innovative take on sculpture no doubt had the potential to repel some and baffle many.

To protect Milo from potential blowback, he'd offered—borderline begged—to help preview, troubleshoot, or advise him. But Milo disavowed the so-called "trap" of outside opinions and refused to budge. Jonathan disagreed but had no choice; he respected the lines Milo had drawn to preserve the impact and purity of his art. In the final days of preparation, even Kara, his benefactor, had been forbidden to enter the exhibit rooms.

Jonathan's thoughts traveled back to the night when Milo showed up on his doorstep. Back then, despite their intense attraction, they'd been relative strangers. Beneath the jokes and quirks, Jonathan was still discovering Milo's complexities, his passion. Milo's heart laid bare, visible on his sleeve, had cracked Jonathan's hardened heart like a damn eggshell. Every time they argued or made up—every moment of every day, he realized—he'd fallen deeper in love with this man. He feared Milo's open heart left him defenseless to predators thirsty for blood. Words had the power to eviscerate. What if the critics picked him apart?

"Dad?"

The sound of Dylan's voice compelled Jonathan back to the present. He inhaled deeply. With his exhale, he banished the doubt. "Hey, kiddo."

The boy scooted himself up onto the couch. "Is it okay if I watch cartoons?"

Jonathan folded his newspaper and turned his full attention to his child. "Yes, until it's time for breakfast."

Dylan nodded blankly, eyes glued to the tube.

Jonathan smiled at the sight of him swimming in his new frog-print pajamas, a size too big and a vast improvement over those he'd outgrown. The kid had sprouted, seemingly overnight, his body stretched out, defined by new hollows and angles. All traces of baby flesh, sadly, gone for good. Unable to resist a moment of togetherness before Dylan morphed into adolescence, Jonathan joined him on the couch. "Ah, *Fractured Fairy Tales*." He draped an arm around his shoulder. "You have excellent taste," he said. "Like father, like son."

The boy curled into his dad. "You like this show?"

"Yep," Jonathan said. "Rocky and Bullwinkle are my favorite."

"Cool. Mine, too."

As they settled into amiable silence, Jonathan recalled the old thirteen-inch black-and-white set he'd found at a Goodwill shop over a decade ago. As a matter of pride, he'd never cared much for TV; he'd taken a common-sense approach, setting limits on Dylan's TV consumption. But when the boy transferred to the Waldorf school, moving into Kara and Kent's upscale condo, Jonathan relaxed his standards. He wasn't proud of it, but the color TV had been a form of leverage. Now, as he ran his fingers through Dylan's tangled hair, breathing in his little-boy scent, he knew it was fleeting. Before long, Dylan would no longer want to cuddle. So, as it turned out, the TV had been a good call.

April 18, 1981
The Afternoon of Milo's Show

Kit rifled through her closet, overwrought with indecision, when she happened upon a forgotten dress from the vintage shop on Fulton. Bingo. With high hopes, she slipped it over her head, tugged at the hem, and adjusted the bodice. She contemplated her image in the bathroom mirror—the dress fit perfectly. It flattered her figure, skimming her shape without clinging. Yet something was off. The lime color that had attracted her now gave her pause. "Fuck," she breathed. There was no denying it. It made her look froggy.

She peeled off the offending dress and flung it to the reject pile. Milo's show was a huge deal. And for the occasion, she had *nothing* to wear. Her New York clothes would never do for a spring evening in California. Kit reached for the pale-blue halter top, a discard from Jesse's wardrobe and her last resort. When Jesse had suggested pairing it with her black midi skirt, Kit resisted. For starters, she didn't think she could pull it off. It was truly more of a "Jesse" look. In short: braless.

She tried it on with the black skirt and had to admit, it didn't look awful. To complete the outfit, a la Jesse's sage advice, Kit added her silver hoop earrings, her best black boots. A glance in the mirror clenched it. Jesse had been right—as usual. Kit drew a breath. Damn, who was that daring babe in the mirror? She admired her reflection, turning this way and that, when a tap at her door startled her. No one. Ever. Knocked.

"Just a sec," she yelled. Then, in a halting stumble across the room, she managed to strip down to her underwear and wrestle on jeans and a sweatshirt.

"Kit? Are you home?" A male voice called to her from outside.

Ben's voice. What was he doing here? In a pointless attempt to tidy her appearance, Kit fiddled with her clothes, then flung open the door. "Hey," she said, out of breath.

Ben offered a hesitant smile. "Hey yourself."

She took a hard look at him. Clean-shaven, hair in place, a suede jacket she hadn't seen before. Clearly Ben had made an effort. Kit felt the blood rush to her cheeks, hotly aware of her own dishevelment. "I wasn't expecting you," she snapped. It came out sounding meaner than she'd intended. "I mean, you said you had to work until six."

Ben smiled, the corners of his eyes crinkling as he gathered both of her hands in his. "Surprise?"

She glanced down at their hands entwined. Hers: small and wan. His: a mechanic's hands, competent and workworn—a doctor's hands, elegant and cool to the touch. "How'd you manage that?"

"I traded shifts with Jennifer. I'm taking her all-nighter."

Jennifer? Ben had never spoken of her. The name evoked a bright, unreasoned pang of jealousy. Kit released a breath, let it go. Given the rigors of his internship, she understood what he'd sacrificed to be here—for her. A decent girlfriend would be grateful, perhaps even thrilled by a surprise visit from her beau. But Kit's emotions, a mishmash of fondness and annoyance, rattled around in her head and wouldn't settle.

As if Ben sensed her confusion, he released her hands. He lifted her chin and looked directly into her eyes. "Are you okay?" he asked. He hesitated for a long moment; his brow creased with concern. "Have I caught you at a bad time?"

A blunt finger of shame poked at the tender spot in Kit's heart. "No, it's fine," she said. She summoned her most convincing smile. "Sorry if I seem weird. I guess you caught me off guard."

Ben avoided her eyes. "I know, I should have called you."

Kit turned her gaze to the porch boards, parched, thirsty for paint. "No. Well, maybe."

He looked to the clouds, as if searching for words. "I just wanted to be there for you, you know." He cleared his throat. "I felt lousy when I broke our date, like I let you down."

Kit rested a palm on his shoulder. "You didn't let me down. Really, I totally get it. Your schedule is insane."

He pulled her close and his lips brushed hers. "Can we salvage this?" he murmured in her ear.

Ben's hands on her waist, his breath in her ear, aroused Kit. Her body responded. She kissed him, scraped her teeth on his lower lip, chapped and dry. The scent of his spearmint coffee breath made her want to draw blood.

Ben groaned. "Should we have dinner before Milo's opening?"

Kit pressed her groin into his and felt him harden. She breathed in his scent, antiseptic and reassuring. What once was new and needed was now repellant. In that instant, she knew it was over. The chemistry was off, the spark gone. "Sure, let's go to dinner," she said.

Ben brightened. "Great. I'll make a reservation at Penelope's. It's a block or two from the gallery."

"The new vegetarian place?"

"Yep."

She couldn't look at him. "I've heard the green curry is good."

"Yeah. The reviews have been great," he agreed.

"Totally."

She blathered on like that, making small talk as if nothing had changed, as if nothing were broken. "What time is it anyway?" she asked.

Ben glanced at his watch. "Quarter to four."

A prickling panic passed through her. "Shit. I had no idea it was so late." Kit's mind raced. After Ben broke their date, Jonathan had invited her to tag along with them. She realized how much she'd been looking forward to Kara's pre-party. But now, like it or not, she was stuck. "I'm going to need time to get ready. Meet you at six?"

Ben agreed. He gave her a quick kiss, then parted.

She kept her sight on Ben as he strode up the path. He turned to wave to her then disappeared from view. With her heart in her throat, she inventoried him: Good-looking. Compassionate. Ambitious. Other than over-extending himself, she couldn't name a fault. Why could she not love him? A troublesome thought occurred to her.

What if it wasn't Ben. What if it was her?

Lately Joe had begun to resurface unbidden and it troubled Kit. He'd shown up in her daydreams, her sleep. In fact, this very morning she'd woken with the halo of a dream, so present, so vivid, she'd questioned her own grasp on reality.

She sees Joe in her new apartment. He is at the stove, smiling and bare-chested, spatula in hand. The intoxicating aroma of pancakes drifts on the air and she hungers for him. He kisses her, his naked flesh warm and tangible as her own. She tastes maple and melted butter on her tongue.

On more than one occasion Kit had picked up the phone, when a tiny inkling of pride stopped her finger from dialing. She'd replace the receiver, her heart thudding like she'd narrowly escaped a tiger in the jungle. Joe's ability to fuck with her head still rankled her, made her horny, made her shiver. Goddamn bottomless longing never went away.

Kit stared into the middle distance and shook her head. No. It definitely was *not* Ben.

April 18, 1981
The Evening of Milo's Show

"Hold still," Jonathan said. He tied Milo's tie for him, then stepped away to admire his handiwork. "Perfection," he concluded.

Milo shrugged. "I'm really not a tie person."

Jonathan released a lengthy exhale, an attempt to regain his composure. At times he felt as if he had two children. "Maybe you could be a tie person for one night. I think it looks smart."

"You would, *Necktie*." Milo said, then snorted at his own wit.

Jonathan disliked his bygone nickname, a pejorative cloaked in humor, the implication—*Necktie*—the uptight fussbudget. He certainly didn't appreciate Milo's resurrecting the insult and having a good cackle at his expense. But this wasn't about him, so he let it go.

Milo cocked his head and gave Jonathan the once-over. "You're looking dapper tonight, Professor." He sidled up close. "Damn good," he breathed.

Jonathan had given a lot of thought to his attire, the navy cashmere sport coat with its subtle windowpane print, the classic white button-down and narrow charcoal tie. He'd quit shaving for days then razored his neckline in a precise manner to create the illusion of stubble by happenstance. In this case he had to agree—he did look damn good. With a coy smile, he took in the glow of Milo's gaze.

Milo ventured again to the mirror to study his reflection. He shook his head as he loosened his tie. "Sorry, Jon. It's just not me. It feels like a noose at my throat."

"Fine," Jonathan breathed. It did no good to argue the point. At least Milo had agreed to wear a decent shirt and jacket. "Suit yourself. Dress like a hobo if that's your preference."

Milo busted out a grin. He straightened the tie and for a long moment studied his image in the mirror. "You're right. I look fucking gorgeous."

Jonathan joined him at the mirror and hugged him from behind. "That you do, darling," he said. His hand drifted down and worked its way into Milo's waistband.

Milo grinned. "We make a cute couple, don't you think?"

Jonathan couldn't help but notice the contrast between them. His compact build, tailored jacket, cropped hair in place. Milo towering over him with that sexy mop of curls. He arched an eyebrow approvingly. "Not bad."

"I dig the stubble, Jon. Very *Miami Vice*."

Jonathan brushed his bristly chin against Milo's smooth cheek.

"Babe," Milo groaned. "That chafes."

Jonathan kissed him soft, then hard. He closed his eyes, ready to dive into the carnal well, when he experienced a weird tingle of electricity in his gut, like a sickness coming over him. He sensed a pair of eyes watching, then dropped Milo like a bag of poisonous snakes. He turned to find Dylan filling the doorway to their bedroom, a plaintive look on his face.

"Dad?"

Jonathan swallowed hard. Shit—shit! Why hadn't he closed the door? "Hey, kiddo, what's up?" he said, aware of the false nonchalance in his tone.

Dylan glanced up at the ceiling. "Nothing. I can't find my other sock."

Jonathan did a double take. He hardly recognized the young man in salt-and-pepper slacks and a dress shirt. He squared his shoulders. "Come on, I'll help you look," he said, a little too brightly.

Dylan nodded. He trailed his father into his bedroom. "I'll check under the bed again," he said.

Jonathan combed through Dylan's sock drawer, as he sifted through his own tangle of emotions. When he'd had "the talk" with Dylan, he tried to be factual, candid. But in the end, he'd felt like an imposter, reciter of clichés.

"Found it!" Dylan cried, holding the sock aloft like a fish on the line.

"Good work, son." Jonathan took a seat on the bed, then patted the space next to him. "Come sit with me for a minute?"

"Don't we have to get ready for Mom's party?"

Jonathan glanced at his watch. "Yeah, but we have a few minutes to spare." He took a deep breath. Where to begin? Sex was fraught, a minefield for adults to navigate, let alone ten-year-old kids. "I want to talk to you about something."

Dylan wore a quizzical frown. "Am I in trouble?"

Jonathan tickled him in the ribs. "You? In trouble? Not a chance." He took another deep breath, biding time and gathering his nerve. "I'll get right to the point. I think you probably saw me kissing Milo just now." He kept his tone neutral. "Am I right?"

Dylan shrugged but said nothing.

Jonathan placed a hand on his shoulder. "I was wondering if you felt uncomfortable about it or if you have any questions for me."

Dylan, visibly squeamish, avoided Jonathan's eyes.

Jonathan persisted. "You know, when grownups love each other, sometimes they want to express their feelings—physically. Most couples are of the opposite sex, like a mom and a dad. But there are also some men who love other men, women who love women."

Dylan rolled his eyes. "Da-ad! I know. I get it. You're my dad and Milo's my other dad." He rolled the runaway sock over his foot, evidently done with his father's monologue.

The tension in the room released like a long-held breath. The kid sure had a way of cutting through the shit straight to the heart of the matter. Children's wisdom, irrefutable—no need to overcomplicate. Jonathan ruffled his hair. "You're one smart kid."

"Dad, where are my shoes?"

One minute a sage, the next a goofball, his boy. Jonathan's chest swelled to aching. "Look in your closet, kiddo."

Jonathan took solace in the knowledge that his child was well, at least for the time being. As a parent, it was his job to prepare his son for the greater world. But it was tricky. In terms of truth telling, he walked a razor's edge and the lines kept blurring. He'd read most of the developmental psychology experts but couldn't reconcile their mainstream advice with his anomalous life. How much information was too much? When did it protect or harm?

The ground beneath his feet was constantly shifting; reverberations echoed in his ears. The San Andreas quivered and snaked beneath the city, but Jonathan knew better. This wasn't an act of God; this was no earthquake. And lately, the rumble had grown louder, the drumbeat of soldiers marching lockstep into battle deafening. Their "war on homosexuality" was gaining momentum. Pitchforks waving, they were coming for him. For Milo. For all the gay men and women. Even in 1981—even in liberal San Francisco, to be gay put him at risk. How did a father explain *that* to his son?

For the time being, he did not.

With effort bordering on Herculean, Jonathan managed to corral everyone out the door and into the car—with time to spare. As he started the engine, he said, "Buckle up, kiddo."

"You don't have to remind me every time. I'm not a baby," he grumbled.

Jonathan glanced back at the boy in his rearview mirror. "Duly noted, my son. Old habits are hard to break."

Milo twisted around for a private confab with Dylan. "Go easy on the old man, okay?" he said in a low tone. In the least-subtle manner possible, he pointed at his own head as he twirled his index finger. Then he turned to Dylan and fake-whispered, "His mind is going."

Dylan giggled in spurts like a broken lawn sprinkler. Then Milo joined in, laughing so hard his eyes watered.

Jonathan chuffed. "I fail to see what's so funny, you two."

"Sorry," Dylan said, gasping for breath.

Jonathan liked it when they kidded him; when they shared a private joke, it pleased him to be left out. Given the complexities of stepparenting, he counted himself lucky for Dylan's nearly seamless acceptance of Milo. Dylan's inner teenager was beginning to emerge, and Milo, a perpetual kid at heart, recognized this. He gave Dylan credit for his growing sophistication. And Milo's penchant for goofiness provided respite from Jonathan's "stodgy old dad" approach to child rearing.

As Jonathan glided through intersection after intersection, green light after green light, he couldn't help but smile. The last glimmer of sunlight cast a luminous aura over the city streets. Colorless clouds shadowed a hint of moonglow. Here he was. In one of the most vibrant cities on Earth with the two people he loved more than life. If God handed him a magical paintbrush, he'd change nothing about this picture. Yet even as the fullness and beauty took his breath away, he couldn't deny the flit of birdwings in his gut. He couldn't escape the noise in his head, the push-pull of his emotions. Milo's fingers, cool and dry to the touch, interlaced with his, a quiet gesture that conveyed everything. Milo saw him. Milo understood. Only when the last of Kara's patrons tricked out—preferably with lighter wallets—would Jonathan breathe easier.

When Jonathan turned onto Powel, he was taken aback by the first red light of the evening. Up ahead, as far as he could see, traffic had come to a standstill. He took his place behind a dinosaur Ford truck. Deflated, he released Milo's hand. "Where did all these people come from? I can't see a thing."

Milo chuckled. "Probably going to my show."

"Could be," Jonathan said. "Might be an accident," he said. The light turned green. He kept his eye on the paralyzed Ford, willing it to budge. As the light returned to red, a lineup of vehicles squeezed in behind them.

Milo moaned. "Looks like we're trapped."

Jonathan stared at the signal for what felt like hours, and finally it went green. "Ah, here we go," he said, as he eased his foot off the brake. Yet again, the Ford failed to advance. This set off a futile honking frenzy. Meanwhile the signal did its red-green thing. Still, no one budged.

Milo exhaled audibly. "I'm going to try to get a better look. He popped his door open, stepped onto the congested roadway and let the door bang shut.

"Dad?"

"Yep?"

"What's happening? Why are we stopped?"

Aware of trepidation in Dylan's voice, Jonathan twisted around to make eye contact. "Probably just a fender bender, kiddo."

Dylan nodded.

"Nothing to worry about, okay?" Jonathan hoped he was right about this, that he wouldn't disappoint. He studied the boy's face, and when he found no trace of distress, returned his gaze to the road. Then the passenger door swung open and Milo dropped down into his seat.

"Could you see anything?" Dylan asked.

Milo banged his door shut, clicked his seatbelt. "Not much. Looks like some happenings up at Washington Square."

Dylan wriggled closer, his ear to the front seat. "Happenings?"

"People gathered for some event," Milo explained.

In that moment, Jonathan sensed movement on his periphery. Indeed, vehicles in the next lane had begun to creep forward. "Hallelujah."

"Can you get over?" Milo asked.

Jonathan glared at the pickup's rear end, immobile as a rock. He squinted into the rearview. "I'll try," he said. He flipped his blinker and began to nose and nudge his way into the next lane. Finally, they were rolling again, albeit turtle slow.

Dylan shuffled and squirmed in his seat. "Will we be late to Mom's?"

Jonathan realized he'd been white knuckling the steering wheel. As he picked up speed, he eased his grip. He checked his watch. "Not late. Fashionably late."

Dylan groaned. "Not funny, Dad."

Milo pointed straight ahead. "Look. It's breaking up now," he said to Dylan.

The traffic knots untangled. As Jonathan's visual field opened, he now discerned the source of the problem. A sign-carrying crowd still clogged the intersection near Washington Square. "Looks like it was some kind of demonstration, but you're right, it's thinning out now."

"Demonstration? What's that?" Dylan chirped.

Presently Jonathan didn't possess the bandwidth to clarify the concept of civil disobedience and drive at the same time. "I'll explain later," he said. "I need to concentrate."

"It's like a protest," Milo offered.

"Okay," Dylan said.

Jonathan braked at the crosswalk as the last few demonstrators snaked their way across the street. Although some still clutched signs, they no longer bothered to hold them aloft. "Smooth sailing ahead, kiddo," he said, summoning his upbeat dad voice. But when he got a closer look at the slogans, his blood ran cold.

Dylan piped up. "Adam and Eve—not Adam and Steve. What does that mean?"

Jonathan gritted his teeth. Why did the kid have to be such a good reader?

Milo shook his head. "Some people are ignorant," he said flatly.

They bypassed the last few stragglers at a painstakingly slow rate. Jonathan imagined Dylan absorbing each slogan in turn, like a kid with a front-row seat at some twisted parade. *We Are the Moral Majority, God Will Prevail, Protect the Children, Family Values*, and so forth. He wracked his brain for some magic formula to erase the ugliness and leave his child unscathed. Then, out of the corner of his eye, he spotted a kid about Dylan's age holding a sign of his own. Jonathan squinted at the message: *Homos Burn in Hell*, framed by a child's hand in Magic Marker orange flames. Bile rose in his throat.

Milo nimbly diverted Dylan's attention from the savagery. "Look Dylan, I can see your mom's street from here," he said, pointing and gesturing animatedly. Then he squeezed Jonathan's shoulder, a gentle reassurance.

Dylan squirmed in his seat to get a good look. "I see it. Cool."

Jonathan glanced in the rearview mirror. He searched Dylan's face for signs of stress, but in his estimation, the boy appeared unharmed. In fact, he wore a sunny, expectant expression as if they were off to Disneyland.

Jonathan set the parking brake. He loosened his grip on the steering wheel. "We made it."

"Good work, Jon," Milo said.

As they strode to Kara's place, Jonathan felt the ocean breeze on his face like a caress. Salty scents—a frothy soup of regeneration and decomposition—life itself drifted on the edges of his awareness. At Kara's doorstep, he glanced over at Milo, achingly handsome in his good clothes. For the first time in memory, he detected reticence in Milo's demeanor, as if he'd just now realized it was too late to back out. "Hey, are you okay?" he asked.

But before Milo had a chance to respond, Dylan rang the doorbell, and it really was too late to cut and run.

As if poised at the ready, Kara yanked the door open. "You made it," she breathed.

Jonathan, or anyone with eyes, could see she was harried. He'd promised to deliver the guest of honor on time, felt like a heel for being late. "Sorry, Kara. We ran into terrible traffic."

For a moment Kara appeared lost in thought. Then, with a wave of her hand, she ushered them in. "Come in. Come in."

Huddled together in the foyer with Milo and Dylan, Jonathan took a good look at Kara, pretty in her aquamarine silk tunic, black cigarette pants and heels. He couldn't help but notice the bluish shadows beneath her eyes, the slight rounding of her middle. His mind drifted back to her pregnancy with Dylan, the first few months fraught with nausea and debilitating fatigue. "How are you feeling?" he wondered aloud.

Kara gave him a weak smile, then swept the perspiration from her brow. "I'm good." Her hand fell to her belly. "All good." She turned to Dylan. "You look so handsome, honey." She shook her head. "So grown up." Then she wrapped him in a mama bear hug until he managed to squirm away.

Milo faked a frown. "What about us? Don't we look handsome?"

Kara chuckled. "That goes without saying. But yes, you both look fantastic."

"You look lovely, too," Jonathan added, perhaps a beat too slow.

Kara leaned in close to Milo. "You'll never guess who's here," she whispered.

Milo gave her a full sparking grin. "Who, pray tell?"

"Jean-Charles Severin. And he's eager to meet you."

Milo looked blank. He shrugged. "Who?"

Kara gave him a playful shove. "Only one of *the* top Paris dealers. Excuse us, won't you?" she said.

Before Jonathan could react, Kara grabbed Milo by the hand and dragged him off. As he watched Milo disappear into the noisy crowd, Dylan yanked on his jacket. "What?" he asked.

"Dad, I know that girl," the boy said with a subtle tilt of his head.

Jonathan spotted a cute little girl in a swingy blue velvet dress. Two long pigtail braids tied with matching blue ribbons hung down her back. She'd decorated the fingertips of one hand with five black olives. He chuckled as she then inhaled them one by one. "Who is she?"

"Lucy. She goes to my school," Dylan said in a hushed tone. Then, with reverence, he added, "She's a fifth-grader."

"Ah. An older woman."

Dylan gave Jonathan an eye roll. "Quiet, Da-ad. She'll hear you."

Jonathan draped his arm over his shoulder. "Maybe you should go say hi."

The boy squared his shoulders. "Okay."

Jonathan's typically reserved son marched straight up to the girl without a backward glance while he stood by agog. Every day the kid surprised him. He eyed Dylan at the cheese table gobbling crackers and chatting to vivacious little Lucy and supposed he should follow suit, that he, too, should mingle. But he couldn't quite muster the energy to move his feet, or the will to partake in the cocktail party convos of the well-dressed and well-heeled.

He found himself wondering about Kara's new condo. No doubt Kent had paid a small fortune for it. Jonathan admitted it was striking, in that modern, angular, stark, impossibly high-ceilinged way. He couldn't explain why he found it off-putting. Perhaps it lacked bones, or maybe it was heart. At any rate, he wouldn't trade his Victorian.

With little desire to socialize, Jonathan felt at sea. But he couldn't loiter in the foyer all evening—or could he? Out of the corner of his eye, he sighted Kent in midstride, and alas, headed his way.

Kent wore a tailored suit and a magnanimous smile. He towered over Jonathan and offered his outstretched hand. "Glad you could make it, Jon."

Jonathan clasped then quickly released the man's hand. "Of course," he said. "Where else would I be?"

Kent grinned. "Indeed," he said, then glanced at his watch.

Was that a Rolex? The gall. The pretense. The height. Envy taunted Jonathan like a schoolyard bully, but he quickly tamped it down. Kent was a decent guy. He was Dylan's stepfather and Jonathan respected him. He may not always like him, but he wanted to like him, so he tried. "Listen, I want to thank you and Kara for taking a chance on Milo. This opportunity means so much to him."

Kent's brow furrowed. "Milo is a remarkable talent." Again, he glanced at his watch. He inhaled sharply. "Excuse me, Jon. It's time."

Jonathan nodded, eyed him as he schmoozed his way to the table.

Kent grabbed a wineglass by the stem, tapped the bowl with a spoon, and waited for the din to settle. "Thank you all for coming this evening," he said. As people wandered and gathered closer, he continued. "Envision Gallery, that is, Kara and I, are honored to introduce an astonishing new talent, Mr. Milo Archer." He rubbed his chin as if thinking. "Europe has already discovered Milo's work, which has been described as witty, didactic, and challenging. We're thrilled to bring his unique vision home—to San Francisco and to all of you."

Polite applause rose from the crowd as Jonathan scanned the room. He noted little Lucy with her pigtails, Dylan, too, and Kara by his side. But where was Milo? Then it dawned on him. Of course. Milo had slipped away to fly solo for his debut, just as he'd said he would. Jonathan pictured him now, adrenaline-fueled, perhaps making last-minute adjustments. He closed his eyes and sent him calming vibes.

Kent forged on. "All of the pieces in the exhibit will be available for sale tonight, unless otherwise noted. And for those of you who haven't already had the pleasure, you'll have a chance to meet Mr. Archer in…" He glanced at his watch then grinned. "…three minutes." Kent paused for the sounds of brief, obligatory laughter. "Ladies and gentlemen, without further ado, we invite you all into the gallery. Please join us as we open our doors to the public. Enjoy the exhibit," he concluded.

While folks fumbled with jackets and purses, Jonathan escaped to the stoop. From there, he glimpsed Kara's gallery across the street and was heartened to see a decent turnout. Amid the throng, he picked out Katherine and Ben at the end of the queue. Scents of kelp and seawater drifted in on a cool evening breeze. Jonathan held still, taking it in. He filled his lungs with salt air, then let his feet carry him.

April 18, 1981
Milo's Show

Ben clasped Kit's hand as they scuttled across the street to the gallery. "The doors haven't opened yet. Told you we'd make it on time," he said.

Milo's night of nights had finally come. Kit's anticipation fizzed and bubbled; her excitement visceral. At the same time, trouble loomed and clouded her mood like a shadow.

Ben kissed her cheek. "You look so pretty tonight," he said.

His kindness irritated her. His very presence got under her skin. His hand, oddly, no longer fit properly with hers. And the more he tried to please her, the greater her repulsion. This made her feel small and mean, too powerful for her own good. "Thanks," she said, even as unspeakable words of derision rattled around in her head.

Kit blamed Ben for her funk. She'd scrambled to get ready and shown up on time for their date at Penelope's, but Ben had kept her waiting. To add to Kit's annoyance, the hostess claimed with a fake apologetic pouty face that she couldn't find their reservation. Out of options and with the clock ticking, Ben had shrugged, then suggested some shitty Denny's clone down the block. Kit, ravenous by then, silently fumed as she scarfed a cheeseburger dripping with grease. Gross. To make matters worse, Ben wouldn't stop apologizing, despite her multiple reassurances. How many times did she have to say it? *They lost the reservation: not your fault.*

Kit had stared at the ketchup juices pooling on her plate, then glanced across the table at Ben. Her stomach roiled with emotional turmoil and bad burger, but in that low moment, clarity arose. Everyone knew breaking up sucked, but indecision worsened and prolonged the misery. Ben had been Kit's fallback, her rebound guy—but he deserved better. By far, the kindest thing would be to let him go.

Ben nudged her. "It's seven fifteen. They're late."

Kit blinked, lost in thought. "What?"

He tapped his watch. "They're late." He studied her. "Are you okay? You seem really distracted."

"Sorry, I guess I am a little." Kit scanned the area for Jesse, who'd said she'd "try" to make it. Instead, she spotted Jonathan. She waved him over.

"Glad I found you two," Jonathan said.

"Me, too," Kit said, relieved for the much-needed third-person buffer. She went in for a quick hug, the scent of his spicy, woodsy, manly cologne not lost on her. "You're looking very sharp tonight."

Jonathan shrugged off the flattery. "I try."

Kit couldn't help but chuckle; the man looked good, and he knew it. "Hey, where's Dylan?" she wondered.

"He's with his mom," Jonathan said, his tone more question than statement. He glanced around. "They should be right behind us."

Ben cut in. "Hey, we're moving."

"Ah, indeed we are." Jonathan grinned. "Ready or not."

Kit took a step forward. She drew a deep breath of the crisp night air. "Ready."

Once folks realized the gallery had opened, the line moved quickly. Kit soon entered the bright lobby, and as she took in the jam-packed lively atmosphere, her senses sharpened. *This was it.* She eyed the many patrons engaged in breezy repartee, the well-dressed aloof—art dealers? The service crew uniformed, invisible, ever at the ready, recalled her waitress days at

Waffle Hamlet. Kit turned her attention to Jonathan. "This is really something, isn't it?" she asked.

Jonathan wore a frozen smile. "Isn't it?"

A good-looking waiter swooped in to offer them each a glass of champagne, which Jonathan declined, and Kit graciously accepted. Another server, also cute, presented a trayful of canapés. Despite the burger-sized lump in her gut, out of kinship for her fellow waitstaff Kit obliged.

Jonathan stepped closer to Kit. "I'm so nervous, I'm sweating through my shirt," he confided.

Kit squinted at Jonathan. This was more than a case of the jitters. It appeared that the dear, sweet man might keel over at any second. "Do you need some air?"

Jonathan shook his head. "Don't want to miss anything."

Kit draped an arm over his shoulder. "Okay, just let me know if you change your mind."

Jonathan lowered his gaze. "Thanks, Katherine."

"Listen, before you know it, this night will be a memory." She patted him on the back. "Have faith, my friend."

"Good advice," he said, then met her eyes. "It appears the student has become the teacher."

"Any time." She held Jonathan's gaze, lingered in the glow of his approval. His affection pleased her, but his approval meant more. To her, on some level, he would always be Professor Wakefield.

Ben wedged in next to Kit. "I thought I lost you for a second," he said, his tone genial. Then he squeezed her hand.

His hand was too warm, his very existence an intrusion. Kit breathed. "I was just talking to Jonathan." She released Ben's hand, picked up her champagne and chugged it. "I'm going to get another. Do you want one?"

Ben wagged his still-full glass, shook his head.

Kit shrugged. "Be right back." She wended her way through the assemblage to a back table replete with bubbly glassfuls. Eureka. One glass she downed on the spot. The second she grabbed for good measure. Kit teetered on her bootheels back to the lobby.

"Katherine!" Kara said.

Kit had met Jonathan's pretty ex-wife a handful of times, and Kara struck her as a down-to-earth, gracious woman. Nevertheless, she always felt a little mousy in her presence. "Hi, Kara."

Kara touched Kit's forearm. "It's nice to see you again. You know, Milo talks about you all the time." Crinkles appeared at the corners of her eyes when she smiled.

"Good things, I hope," Kit said. Rote. Dopey. A line from the small-talk handbook.

Kara tossed her long braid over her shoulder, leaned in like they were old friends sharing a secret. "He adores you."

Kit decided she liked Kara. Her gaze fell to Dylan, head bent over some beeping handheld game. Unable to resist, Kit ruffled his hair. "Hey, aren't you going to say hi?"

The boy lifted his head a fraction of an inch. "Hi."

Kit persisted. She bent at the waist to meet him at eye level. "Where'd you get that game?"

"It's Lucy's," Dylan said, still not looking up.

Kara tilted her head toward the young girl.

"Ah," Kit said. "Cool." In truth, she couldn't fathom the appeal. Beyond all doubt, these little electronic gizmos were destined to fizzle out like pet rocks.

Kara rolled her eyes.

Kit excused herself. She scanned the room in search of Ben. Bathroom, she figured. She leaned against the wall, sipped her champagne, and people watched, hoping he would spot her in the crowd. But after a short while, her attention flagged. Kit wandered from the bustle into a quiet passageway. Curious, she continued around a corner, where she discovered Jonathan and Milo. Kit secretly studied them as they shared a quiet moment.

On cue, Milo the mind reader glanced up. He locked eyes with hers.

Kit waved.

Milo's impossible grin—too big for his face, childlike, expansive, generous—radiated across the room directly into her heart. Her gaze fixed on the face of her dear, goofy friend as the houselights lowered and Milo slowly vanished in the dusky light. Out of nowhere, a distant, steady drumbeat caught her ear. The sound gained momentum—faster, louder. Disoriented, Kit groped her way back to the lobby, to the light. She found the lobby packed with bodies that rocked and swayed to the beat. As she joined the throng, the beat thundered in her ears, resonating into her very core. Then abruptly, the drumming stopped.

In the silent nothingness, the slightest movement or whisper was magnified. Kit breathed in the stillness. As the houselights gradually brightened, the exhibit doors glided open. With a murmur of collective awe, the crowd began to shuffle forward. Kit took her place in line but as she approached the entrance, the doors shut.

Then Kara appeared. "Please be patient, everyone. The anteroom can only accommodate about twenty people at a time."

Kit frowned. She searched the room for a familiar face; Jonathan or Milo, even Dylan would do.

For that matter, where was Ben?

But deep in her bones, she already knew. Relief, like cool rain, washed over her.

Ben had been driving her nuts all evening, exhausting her patience, demanding attention like a puppy at her heels. Kit was glad to be rid of him. Indeed, the mere thought of his presence enraged her. The outer doors swished open, snapping Kit back to the present. In this charged moment, she felt her heart beating in her chest. On the brink of witnessing her dearest friend's debut, the last thing she needed was Ben sucking up all the airspace. She needed to be free to experience this moment on her terms. Without a backwards glance, she crossed the threshold alone.

Kit squeezed into tight room with about dozen other people, a claustrophobic's nightmare. She folded her arms tight across her chest and willed herself to shrink but couldn't avoid rubbing shoulders. The rank odor of stale cigar smoke made her nose twitch. She stifled a sneeze as she fixed her gaze on the glowing red emergency exit sign above the door.

Sounds of a scratchy record emanated from some unseen speaker, then a disembodied voice launched: *You are entering a multisensory, multidimensional presentation. We ask that you advance single file through the corridor, then continue at your own pace. For an optimal experience, as intended by the artist, please follow the directional arrows. Thank you.*

Yet another attendant opened yet another sliding door. Kit took her place in line and filed into a dimly lit, narrow hall. As patrons slowly herded into first exhibit hall, she couldn't contain her impatience, resenting those ahead of her, taking their sweet time. After an ice age or two, at last, Kit's turn came.

But as she turned the corner, she confronted yet another closed door. An eternity ensued and then the door slid open, granting her passage. Kit stepped into a small white room. As the door closed, she breathed in the blessed moment of solitude, then understood Milo's intention. Each guest was meant to be here alone. Her gaze turned to the sole display, a curious little artifact in a glass case. **Kit circled the glass case to inspect the work from every angle. Now, it was her turn to take her sweet time.**

At first glance, the object on the pedestal reminded her of the intricate miniature Native American baskets she'd seen in books and museums. Upon closer inspection, she realized it had been woven not from grass, but wire. The impossibly tiny basket held an even tinier egg. Taking a closer look at the egg, she recognized the translucence of sea glass, one of Milo's favorite mediums. She pondered the delicate pale blue egg juxtaposed with the rust-colored wire, so simple, yet so effective. For reasons she couldn't explain, it took her breath away.

Lost in thought, she meandered around the corner into a huge bright, open room. As her eyes adjusted to the light, she shuffled into a labyrinth of basket nests. Kit shuffled slowly, taking care to study each nest in turn, each one more astounding than the last. Large and small, whimsical and disturbing, Milo's nests were fashioned from all manner of material—cracked eyeglasses, watchbands, string. Coke cans, rusted bike chains, broken pencils. Shoelaces, toothpaste tubes, spark plugs, dental floss. Dryer lint? Like a kid on Easter morning, Kit hunted for sea glass eggs, hidden gems.

Kit moved along to the next exhibit, and for the first time encountered other visitors milling about. She joined the crowd, pausing to gaze at actual eggshells, some with hairline cracks. Hummingbird's eggs. Robin's eggs.

Ostrich eggs. Then she chuckled at a series of plastic eggs in various states of hatching. Plastic dinosaur babies emerging from giant plastic eggs. Rubbery snakes and miniature farm animals. Chocolate eggs cracking out tiny plastic human babies. Absurd and brilliant.

Kit slowly made her way to the main exhibit hall, and her eyes practically fell out of her head as she gaped at a confusion of outsized nests. They were, in a word, outrageous. She envisioned Milo dressed in stained coveralls, his crazy curls and welding goggles. How his mind conceived this beautiful, somehow logical mayhem, she had no idea. And why nests?

She started with the smallest creation in the room, a jumble of kitchen utensils, driftwood, and sea glass, an echo of Milo's windchimes—his gift to her. She closely examined each individual part. But as her gaze softened, it transformed into something whole. The beauty and complexity touched an emotion she couldn't name.

A series of egg-shaped mosaics hung on the wall. She investigated them up close—the individual bits of glass, seashells, pebbles, metal fragments, eggshells—then stood back for the full effect. Milo's diverse works deeply moved her; they challenged and confused her. Taken separately, each distinct work possessed merit, she thought. But, taken as a whole, the collection was so much greater than its parts. A light switched on in Kit's head—she understood. This was more than Milo's creation, more than a 3D expression of his heart and mind. This *was* Milo.

Kit meandered down another corridor, deep in thought, when a gentle wind stopped her in her tracks. The sensation of wind in her hair, the sounds of wind instruments called her to the final exhibit. For a long moment, she stared agog at fishing lures, paperclips, rebar, nuts and bolts, kitchen gadgets, a child's toy truck—all magically suspended in midair. The light played tricks and changed color, casting shadows that danced and flickered on the white walls. Upon closer inspection, Kit discovered that translucent fishing line, not magic, held the objects in midair. But this awareness didn't explain the tears in her eyes.

Kit stepped outside into the night, then hoofed it back to the restaurant, knowing with certainty Ben's car would be gone. Penelope's was still open, though much quieter now. She considered a couple seated near the lighted window sharing a late supper. Kit imagined them in love, happy.

If the restaurant hadn't lost Ben's reservation, would tonight have turned out differently? Would she have wanted it to turn out differently? She didn't think so.

She jumped into her VW Bug, started the engine. As she made her way home, she wished Ben had never given her this car, though in some ways, having wheels had saved her. But she'd also felt indebted to him, and it wasn't about the money. She didn't have the right currency to repay his brand of generosity because there were strings attached.

The moment Kit got home, she dialed Ben straightaway.

"Hello?" he said, his voice thick.

"Sorry, did I wake you?"

"Kind of."

She flopped down on her bed. "Ben, I want to apologize about tonight." Kit contemplated the ceiling. "But I think we need to talk."

"Yeah," he said, cutting her off. "I don't think we should see each other anymore."

Mini acrobats turned somersaults in her belly. "What?"

Ben cleared his throat. "I'm pretty sure you heard me."

Kit breathed heavily into the phone. "Wait. What are you saying?" she asked, though she knew the answer.

They spoke in circles for an hour or so, around and around. Kit tried to convince Ben to reconsider. She backtracked. Somehow, now that it was his idea, the breakup felt wrong. "I know I haven't been sensitive to the demands of medical school and your work."

But Ben had made up his mind. "Kit, it's not about that."

Kit finally conceded, too drained to carry on and too tired to care. "Okay, then. Let's make it official. Anyway, I'm exhausted. I need to go."

Now that it was really, truly over, she felt only relief. Milo's show had inspired her to make her own magic. She realized she had much to be grateful

for, much to look forward to. In fact, she'd never been more ready to move on —
that is, after a good night's sleep.

"Kit?"

She sighed. "Yeah?"

Ben cleared his throat. "I need to talk to you about your friend Milo."

"What about him?" she asked, feeling mean and defensive. "What do you
want to tell me?"

"He doesn't look well," he said. "Promise me you'll make him see a
doctor, okay?"

Kit closed her eyes to shut out Ben's words, to shut out Ben. The silence
crackled, filling her ears with static. "Fine. Whatever. I promise."

That Night

Jonathan pulled into the driveway, home at last.

"What a night," Milo said, a dreamy look on his face. "I'm fried. I could sleep for a week."

Jonathan unbuckled his seatbelt, turned around in his seat. "Looks like you're not the only one," he said. The vision of his slumped, slumbering child brought a sweet stab of nostalgia. All the years gone by. Countless times he'd carried his little limp body, always heavier than expected, into the house and tucked him into bed. It crossed his mind now to simply scoop Dylan into his arms. But at age ten, weighing in at 72 pounds, his son no longer qualified as little. "Hey, kiddo," he said, nudging him.

Dylan stirred. "What?"

"Wake up, son. We're home."

Dylan mumbled something incomprehensible, then opened his eyes. With a yawn, he sat up. "Okay, I'm awake."

Jonathan unbuckled the boy's seatbelt for him. "Let's go," he said. He couldn't help but smile as Milo, then Dylan, crawled out of the car and trudged up the front steps. Jonathan followed them to the porch. He slipped the key into the lock, and as the door swung open, Zeke streaked between his shins into the house.

Milo hung inside the foyer and with a yawn kicked off his shoes. "Boys, I'm off to bed," he declared. "Goodnight," he said, bleary-eyed, as he trailed down the hall. Then he turned back. "Thank you for being my people."

"Goodnight," Dylan sang.

Jonathan tucked Dylan in with the cat and gave them both a goodnight kiss. In keeping with his routine, he double-checked the front door, then headed through the kitchen to ensure the back door, too, had been locked. He glanced out the kitchen window to Katherine's studio, her light on at this late hour. For unknown reasons, this gave him pause. He'd grown closer to her in recent months, yet much about her remained a mystery. And lately she'd seemed a bit distracted and at times detached. Who was Katherine Hilliard? Or more precisely, who was she becoming?

With a faraway smile, he recalled that January day. His little foundling, in need of a home. He'd felt like her savior, her hero. Oh, how his chest had puffed. He shook his head at his own deep, seemingly endless well of male ego. Funny how tables turned. Funny that he'd come to depend on her, to love her like his own.

Jonathan yawned deeply, headed into the bedroom, undressed, and fell into bed. He stroked Milo's curly head. "I'm so proud of you," he said.

Milo stretched and wrapped Jonathan's body with all four limbs. He sniffed Jonathan's head. "My sweet, sweet man."

"Do you know how many pieces you sold tonight?"

"Not exactly."

"I spoke to Kara. A lot of the smaller ones sold."

Milo yawned. "Hm."

"She also said a dealer made her an offer on the finale. You're going to be rolling in green, my love."

"I'm tuckered, Jon," Milo said, fading out. "Sorry. Let's talk tomorrow."

Jonathan kissed him. "As you wish."

Milo rolled to the opposite side of the bed and burrowed in for the night.

Jonathan lay still, his eyes on the ceiling as he listened to the sounds of Milo drifting off to sleep. He contemplated this beautiful, snoring man next to him in bed. Milo had, once again, astonished him. His work defied description, category, or genre, and Jonathan was still trying to wrap his head around all he'd seen. Milo didn't fit into any box; in fact, Milo broke the box.

Milo's triumph felt like the start of something, some wondrous, unstoppable force. He knew for certain he and Milo were bound to ride the wave together. Together, they would leap into the vast unknowable and all the extraordinary days that lay ahead. Contentment washed over him, or maybe it was faith.

Epilogue
December 1988

Jonathan pounded out the chicken breasts, chopped the herbs, and readied the stockpot for pasta. He warmed the olive oil, dry white wine, and lemon juice, then stirred in a handful of capers. A sprinkle of salt, a dash of pepper, a good-sized lump of butter, each step of Dylan's favorite recipe a mediation. He still couldn't quite wrap his head around it—his kid was in college now. And tonight they'd celebrate his homecoming.

He'd been pressed for time when Kara offered to collect Dylan from the airport. But as he glanced at his watch for what felt like the hundredth time, he wished he'd tagged along. Ah, well. Nothing to be done about it now. He ambled into the dining room to check his table setting with a critical eye. With care, he adjusted a water glass by a fraction of an inch, refolded one napkin, straightened a fork. He stepped away to take in the full effect and smiled as he admired his handwork.

He turned his focus to the Christmas tree, wrapped in popcorn garlands, strung with glowing white lights. It would do, he mused. But alas, like all predecessors, it paled in comparison to the legendary giant. As Jonathan envisioned that ridiculous hulk of a tree, he chuckled aloud. With a faraway smile, he recalled the long-ago morning, four of them scrunched into the cab of Milo's pickup, headed north to Zander's Farm. That golden milestone

212

Christmas—his first with Milo. Bathed in rose light. A daguerreotype, unchanging.

And Katherine had been there, too. For some reason, she'd been on Jonathan's mind lately. He admitted that without her constant presence, he would have fallen apart. Her support for Milo—for him—had held them together, especially at the end. He shook his head, remembering. And she'd continued to surprise him with her grit and capability.

It was a shame she couldn't make it for Christmas this year. These days, her journalism compelled her to travel around the globe. It had been her series, The Faces of AIDS, that launched her Chronicle column into syndication. His heart swelled with a kind of fatherly pride when he thought about how far that girl had come since their holiday excursion to the tree farm.

When was that? Seven? No, it had been eight years ago now.

Memories seeped beneath his skin, liquid, unbidden. Closely guarded, private archives, locked away. It pained him to remember, pained him to forget. He lay a palm at his sternum above the tender spot deep in the pith of his heart. Somehow, he'd been fooled by the promise of a future, limitless lazy hours ahead of them—too many to conceive.

How he'd clung to that illusion.

In the early days following Milo's exhibition, Jonathan figured the poor guy had simply overdone it. Weeks later, when Milo's fatigue worsened, Katherine showed up with foul-tasting herbal teas and other potions from the health food store. Enter the doctors with their puzzled looks and rounds of antibiotics. Nothing worked. Milo's low-grade pneumonia symptoms persisted; his lesions refused to heal.

The rest of it had blurred in Jonathan's memory. There'd been Milo's hospitalization, followed by the GRID (Gay-Related Immune Deficiency) diagnosis, a pointedly cruel death sentence. Milo continued to suffer while Jonathan, helpless, pretended all would be well. Even as he'd spooned vanilla ice cream past Milo's desiccated lips, Jonathan denied the visual evidence. Even as the vitality drained from Milo's body, Jonathan refused to see.

In quiet moments at Milo's bedside, his thoughts circled back to his friend, Beth. Her son, Jamie had been a young man, torn from his mother's arms, ripped from the very fabric of the universe, and left to float forever in the ether. Yet Beth had managed to carry on, to utter words, to walk upright. Jonathan refused to acknowledge Milo's decline, so like Jamie's. At times, the burden of pretending felt so heavy it threatened to crush him. Thinking of Jamie's death, he'd head into Dylan's room to bury his nose in the boy's hair, inhaling his boy funk like a tonic.

Funny, how the mind played tricks. Funny, how his magical thinking had no limit. Even as the hospice nurse had taken his hand and led him away.

He coughed out a laugh, shook his head to shake the memory.

It had been Louise, the social worker, who'd made him face reality. As he'd plodded forward into a Milo-less future, Louise's grief counseling support group had helped him feel less alone. And yes, he'd seen wisdom in Kübler-Ross's theory, however, thus far he'd failed to graduate to stage five—acceptance.

But he was working on it.

He stepped outside and glanced below to the street—still no sign of Dylan. A chill breeze caressed his cheek, bringing Milo's windchimes to life. Like it was yesterday, he pictured Katherine atop the stepladder. She'd hung them at his doorstep for safekeeping, she'd said, when her work compelled her from San Francisco, from her little place up on Telegraph—from him.

Jonathan shivered, then headed indoors to escape the chill. Katherine's presence in his life had been a blessing, he mused, as he wandered back to the kitchen. Their mutual love for Milo, like a secret club, an abiding bond. Katherine knew Milo's quirks, his nonsense. She knew his grin, his frown, his knowing expression. She knew that Milo had drilled the deepest recesses of Jonathan's soul, his shame, his strengths, his humanity. She knew because Milo had loved her, too.

When he'd given up all hope, it had been Katherine who'd helped him realize a singular truth. Milo's life had ended, but Jonathan's had not. With her prodding, he'd tasked himself to get on with the business of living. Anything less than his living his best life would only dishonor Milo's spirit. Thus, he'd carried on, one foot in front of the other—for Milo, until the better days outnumbered the difficult, unbearable days. Through it all, his saving grace had been Dylan. His refuge, writing, and long, long, walks.

Upon completion of his novel—part agony, part catharsis—he'd fired Zimmerman, then promptly hired his old friend Zelda, returned from her hiatus. It paid off. Who knew readers hungered for a story set in San Francisco in the eighties with a gay protagonist? *City of Dreams* became an instant best seller, to his ongoing bafflement and joy.

Jonathan, approaching fifty now, had eclipsed his aspirations. If given a choice, he wouldn't trade his life. All the love and pain, intertwined. There had been a few men since Milo, friends mostly, whose intellect or humor turned his head. He didn't find his life lacking and wasn't searching for romance, though he hadn't ruled out the possibility.

A sudden clatter out on the front porch caught his attention, then the ring of the doorbell. Zeke, the scrawny old cat, accompanied Jonathan as he threw open the door to the sight of his son, so handsome, eyes bright. Little Jillian, now three, grinned at Jonathan as she pressed a pudgy finger to the doorbell button again and again. Kara's eldest daughter, Gracie, rolled her eyes. Kent behind Kara, a hand on her shoulder.

Dylan stepped inside and dropped his duffle bag to the floor. He met Jonathan's eyes, then gave him a crushing hug. "Hey, Pop, it's good to see you."

Dylan, a head taller than his dad, looked different, though Jonathan couldn't say why. He wondered. Had he also changed in his son's eyes? "You, too, kiddo," he said, then with a start, remembered the others. "Come in, come in, everybody." He hung back to watch as Dylan's adoring little sisters skittered away to find their gifts under the Christmas tree. Jonathan's sedate hallway echoed with the pleasing meld of voices, sounds of children's laughter in the air. How good it felt to have a houseful.

Author's Note
June 2021

In *Larkspur*, a sequel to *Heliotrope*, a trio of bygone friends converge in San Francisco.

I chose San Francisco in the early eighties because I wanted to capture a pivotal moment in history marked by unforeseen change. "Before" times, if you will. I would argue that the sociopolitical conservatism of the eighties closely resembles today's right-leaning political extremism. One step forward—two steps backlash.

In June of 1981, a baffling illness known first as Kaposi's sarcoma, a rare and often rapidly fatal form of cancer, was first diagnosed in forty-one homosexual men. In reference to that time, Dr. Anthony Fauci recalled an early CDC report in the summer of 1981 that mentioned "cases of strange infections and tumors in male homosexuals in the New York City area and in California— LA and San Francisco."

Although documented cases of AIDS existed prior to 1970, its outbreak within the gay population ignited an already-smoldering anti-gay fire. The religious right demonized those stricken and perpetuated rumors about the so-called gay disease. Gross medical negligence and antipathy for AIDS patients, largely gay men, led to widespread suffering and death.

The crisis in San Francisco and other cities sparked a wave of national protests, with powerful and far-reaching impact. The global gay rights movement of the 1980s paved the way for contemporary LGBTQIA activism. I began writing *Larkspur* years ago, before the term COVID had entered our lexicon, before the 2016 election . . . before. The completion of my first draft, unbeknownst to me, coincided with the fortieth anniversary of the AIDS epidemic.

In 2021, we face another crossroads in human history. Another virulent virus, politicized.

216

Change is inevitable, hardwired into every living cell and quantum particle on earth. We know that early humans evolved over millennia, gradually, with one generation resembling the next. However, more recently, the advancement of technology has accelerated human evolution. Within a single generation we are fundamentally changed—cognitively, chemically, biologically, and in aspects we've yet to reckon with.

Please forgive my oversimplification, but as an elder, I've earned the right to an occasional grumpy rant. I may not always recognize it these days, but I still love this complex country of ours. I still have hope for this fragile, remarkable planet we are blessed to share.

References

Altman, Lawrence K. Rare *Cancer Seen in 40 Homosexuals*, New York Times Archives, 1981

Jones, Cleve. *When We Rise: My Life in the Movement.* Hachette, 2016.

Ryan, Christopher, *Civilized to Death: What Was Lost on the Way to Modernity.* Simon and Shuster, *2019*

JC Miller is a freelance essayist and the author of five novels, including the best-selling Vacation. A California native, wildfire refugee and table tennis enthusiast, JC resides in Portland, Oregon.